The D Diary

The Story of a Girl's Struggle Through Depression & God's Transforming Power

Jana L. Letterman

It is with great pleasure I recommend Jana Letterman, her book "The D Diary" and her site www.ALightFilledLife.com. In one swoop she is both student and teacher. Her life lessons become yours and for those battling with depression, brings great relief. Those embracing her journey no longer must suffer alone.

Because we cannot see depression, most suffer in silence. Eighty percent of those suffering do not seek treatment. THIS is exactly why a personal journey like Jana Letterman's is so important to tell, and make available to those suffering depression. Through Jana's journey, those who suffer depression know they are not alone.

What a gift Jana brings to all through her very real words. I am privileged to have watched her journey and know, *without a doubt* she is brave beyond words.

Brenda McClain, Special Projects Director, Hoffman Media

The D Diary is a perfect blend of what people need to read who suffer from depression and what people need to read and understand who have a loved one battling depression. Jana also manages to blend a very personal and unique autobiographical account with words of wisdom and encouragement for people who have "been there" and need to know that there is hope. She also mixes very smoothly the stories of other people as they touched her story, but at the same time she refuses to cast blame or shame on any of them. I feel that this is an important book for others who have had tragedies (even long hidden ones) in former generations of their family and are having trouble making sense of inherent but inexplicable sadness. Jana's book calls us to ask the questions, "Why am I the way I am? Where do these feelings come from? Is there any hope for me?" This is a strong and insightful work worthy of the effort it might take to travel emotionally through it.

Dan Knight, Minister of Adult Discipleship at Overland Park Church of Christ and the Author of Grace Gifts

Jana has transferred her life experiences onto the written page and invites her readers to share her family's past and the spiritual journey she has taken, both at the side of that family, and, sometimes, in spite of it. She has taken the skeletons from the closet, put flesh on the bone, and woven a narrative that includes her past as well as her present, measuring her spirit-led walk in specific steps that include psychological insight and spiritual growth. Jana has poured heart and soul into her book until it reaches the brim to overflowing. She has shared herself and her insights here, and each reader will find blessings in her story.

Tim McNeese, Professor, York College & Author

DEDICATION

This book is dedicated to my parents,
brother and uncle and their undying love,
faith, support and bravery.

ACKNOWLEDGMENTS

The development of this book has been a long journey filled with grief, acknowledgement and tears. It has also been a journey of hope and light. It has only been possible because of the support and courageous spirit of my family and friends. I am forever thankful and gracious.

Grandpa
For as many things as I do not understand about my grandpa there are many things I clearly know. He was a man who was devoted to his wife and family.
He was faithful and a constant provider.

While, I do not understand his choices I know that he had great and positive influences on countless family members and friends. He shared memories, laughter and good times with many. I may not have shared many of those experiences with him but I know the moments are precious to others.

My hope is to one day talk to grandpa in heaven and better understand his hurt and his decisions. My other hope is that through sharing this experience others might learn, find strength and be encouraged to help each other along the way.

CONTENTS

1) The Day We All Changed

I'm sitting on a cold pew surrounded by family. Everything is stale and cold. There are tears and you can hear the sounds of weeping. I'm not sad and no tears fall from my eyes. Anger is the only feeling running through my veins, through my heart. So much anger, it's literally oozing out of my pores and my body is shaking. How could someone be so selfish? One by one family and friends tell of fond memories of my grandpa. Why do I not have any good memories?

My mind is racing. Thoughts fly up and down like a rollercoaster turning and sprinting causing chaos in my mind. I try to justify the brutality and reality of suicide. I try to logistically make sense of this heart-breaking puzzle. No matter how hard I try, the pieces do not fit. There's nothing logical about suicide. How does one get to that point? How do they cross that line? Do they even care about those they leave behind? Do they think about them at all?

My skin is crawling. Thousands of tiny ants are marching up and down every part of my body. I just want to run away. It's all too much to handle. Too difficult. How does one slip a rope around their head and simply let go of their life? How can it really be that bad?

Without knowing, sitting on that frigid pew the day of my grandpa's burial, steam funneling out my ears filling the funeral home marked the day my heart officially disconnected from my body. In the years to follow depression would slowly seep into my veins in the form of melancholy, isolation and dread. Its movement would creep along slower than a turtle but steadily and determined to become part of my being. During major transitions it has reared its ugly head with power and influence over my life. Its effects have been manipulative and commanding while being sly and elusive.

Like any tragedy it hits your heart like an anchor sinking you to the depths of the ocean. But, you get up in the morning and go to work. You do the laundry. You run errands. You even start to laugh. Day by day the load gets lighter and it's easier to breathe. The weight slowly lightens. Pretty soon you don't even realize that you've drifted up and you're now floating. However, there's still an anchor tied to my little toe. I'm just not for sure what it is or why it's there. Thus begins my own journey with depression.

Depression, like diabetes or heart disease can be genetic, traveling from sister to brother, from grandmother to mother to child, leaching into every generation. This accurately describes my family's history of depression. My sibling, uncles, cousins, parents and grandparents have all suffered from depression in various forms and to various degrees. Some have learned to live with the condition and have found relief through support systems, the medical community and from God. Others have not. Both my maternal and paternal grandfathers succumbed to depression and suicide. A simple rope was all that was needed to end their lives.

How does this happen? Why is relief so hard to grasp and hold onto? Why do others never find relief? I would need more fingers than my hands provide to count off the friends and family I know who have committed suicide. I do not know the answers. I only know my experiences and feelings imprinted on my heart.

The goal of this book is to draw upon practical and proven methods to achieve a life without depression, learn to use the tools God has given us to live with depression, and give insight and help for those with depression. Throughout the book I draw upon my own experiences in dealing with this disease and illustrate how all things are possible if you believe and allow God to lead you.

Whether you suffer from depression, need help through a rough time or simply find possibilities in the encouragement I know you'll find hope in this book. And, don't we all need a little hope! My hope is you'll walk away with tools, goals and desires rooted in the word of God, enabling you to live the happy life He intended for you.

2) Learning Contentment & Forgiveness From Grandpa

I remember the alarming terror in my grandmother's voice. Her screams reached out of the answering machine clinging to my throat and took my breath away. I was 22, just recently graduated from college but still living at home with my mother and father. No one else heard these screams that are etched into my memory. It's weird because I don't remember her words. Only the screams. The noise. The pitch. The terror in her voice. I remember running to my parents. I remember not knowing what was wrong. But, I can remember the screams as if it was yesterday. I still hear the screams at night sometimes. They come to me in dreams. I've never told anyone that. I guess it is part of the secrecy of depression. The shame of it.

I soon learned that my grandfather had committed suicide. I think saying it that way almost makes it okay. The word suicide softens the veracity of the act. What he really did was slide a rope around his neck and suffocated the breath of his life away. On a Sunday morning in the month of June he chose to make no more choices. He did this knowing Grandma would be left to deal with his choice when she returned home from church. It was his choice. How can someone do that? I know this is something I will never understand.

As a kid, I never really knew my grandpa. As an adult, I still do not know him. He was always quiet and distant. He was a man of few words. His elusive and quiet manner translated to bad moods, and as a kid in elementary school it made me afraid of him. As an adult, I now know that in some ways his expression or lack thereof were signs of his depression. I know this because I've studied my family history and I've been on my own journey. Depression doesn't always come in the form of sadness and tears. It can take over your life in the form of anger and isolation. It can clench onto your motivation and devour your drive to nurture relationships. It innocently takes away your desire to live.

The days following my grandpa's death are kind of a blur. I remember everyone being sad. I was only angry. I didn't get it. I still do not understand. The sadness spoke through silence, not words. How can someone can be so selfish? How can someone inflict so much pain to those who love them most? Even knowing that I suffer from depression I don't get it. Why was grandpa depressed? Why couldn't he decide to control his depression instead of letting it control him? Why couldn't he simply choose to be happy?

Being happy starts and ends with you. It's your choice. It's your decision. Some people feel they don't deserve to be happy. Sometimes Satan uses guilty feelings about past transgressions to control our outlook on life. However, this isn't what God wants for you and for me. He wants you to be happy and let the past go. He doesn't remember the past so why should you dwell on it? *"If we freely admit that we have sinned and confess our sins, He is faithful and just and will forgive our sins and continuously cleanse us from all unrighteousness,"* 1 John 1:9 AMP.

Others feel like they just don't measure up and continue to judge themselves against others and worldly standards. But, God has made us each unique with our own weaknesses and strengths so it makes no sense to judge each other because we are all different! And, we are each made in the image of God. *"…and to put on the new self, created after the likeness of God in true righteousness and holiness,"* Ephesians 4:24 NAS.

There is absolutely no reason or logic to feel inadequate. A persistent inadequate feeling of self is like a slap in God's face. It's like saying to God, "I know you made me and I'm like you but that still isn't good enough." Don't you think it makes God sad when we have these feelings?

God has given you the opportunity to be uniquely you! Measuring up to others is a moot point. Ask God to help you explore, learn and use your strengths in every way possible, in every day.

It was only a few days after my grandpa's funeral when I was hit in the chest again. I was talking to my mom and dad when the subject of my other grandpa (my father's dad) came up in conversation. He had died when I was in second grade. I vividly remember him being sick and in the hospital. I remember me and my brother getting in trouble for chasing each other up and down the endless halls and elevators in the hospital. I remember the day my grandfather died. I remember sitting on the pew in the funeral home. I remember the smell of grass, the dirt, and the freshly cut flowers at the cemetery.

What I didn't remember was how he died. I always thought cancer had taken his life. This is the memory etched into my brain. However, on this day only hours after my one grandpa committed suicide I found out that my other grandpa had also committed suicide so many years before. Cancer had not taken my grandfather's life. He had chosen to take it himself. I had absolutely no clue. I had lived nearly twenty years without this knowledge. I felt like my world was crumbling beneath my feet. I could see the terror and concern in my parents' eyes. They thought I knew. We were all stunned.

I was utterly shocked and confused. I felt horrible for my parents because they sincerely thought I knew. My mind couldn't keep anything straight. I couldn't rationalize either of their decisions and I felt like I was getting sucked into a tornado. My mind was spinning through a funnel of confusion and there was no end in sight. I wanted to rationalize everything and come to a logical conclusion or explanation but so few things in life are really black and white. Instead they are a million shades of gray. My parents had never intentionally kept this from me.

I guess I was too young to comprehend the severity of the situation and Grandpa's true cause of death. So, in one very long life-changing week I found out that both of my grandfathers committed suicide. Both chose a rope. One in the shed and one on a cherry tree. Both left their wives, children and friends to deal with that which they couldn't deal. Both gruesome, violent acts. Both haunt our family to this day and always will.

I was in search for answers. I needed to know why. I needed to know how I was connected. I needed peace amongst the chaos of my feelings and thoughts. Ironically depression can give a person peace with all of these things. Depression disconnects you from all of your feelings. It can void you of thoughts. It takes away your need for answers, logic and interaction.

Depression builds vulnerability within your soul hidden by impending walls of protection. God can help you climb through, over or around that wall. It's ironic that when you feel the most lost and vulnerable that God uses the situation to teach and mold. He pulls you through the situation, no matter how dire the circumstance. I know God has been molding me since the day I heard my grandmother's screams. It's unconditionally wonderful how God sends you messages when you need them and they are always right on target. One of my favorite songs is, "It is Well with My Soul". Every time I hear this song it moves the deepest depths of my heart and reminds me that God is watching over and protecting me through all of life's trials. If you don't know the history of the song and its creation it is a beautiful but tremendously sad story.

Several years ago when I was living in Kansas City, the church choir sang a rendition of this song and then told about the author and the moments in his life that served as the inspiration for this song. It is a story of unbelievable tragedy and heartache, a sorrow many of us would be unable to bear. As you face hurdles and sadness in your life reflect and draw hope from this song and its story. I hope it gives you strength and contentment.

Here's the story. Life was going pretty well for Horatio G. Spafford, the author of the song. He was a lawyer in Chicago during the 1860's where he had built a life for his wife, Anna and their five children, one boy and four girls. He probably didn't have much to complain about. He had a solid career, he and his wife were well known and prominent within the community, he had a huge and healthy family and he was a believer in God.

Have you ever been at a point in your life when you think things can't get any better? And then you're hit in the face with a string of bad luck and tragedies? Many of us have struggled down this path and in 1870 Horatio experienced his string of tragedies. Then his only son was struck by scarlet fever and passed away at the young age of four. Unfortunately, this was only the beginning. In 1871, the famous "Chicago Fire" struck the city and with it took numerous real estate investments along the shores of Lake Michigan belonging to Horatio.

Suffering now from the passing of their son and financial loss, the Spafford family struggled to move on. In 1873 the entire family decided to travel across the seas to England for a holiday and also meet up with their dear friend, DL Moody, one of the great evangelists of the time. The family made the journey from Chicago to

New York to board the boat set for England and at the last minute Horatio was called back for an imminent business need. Turning around to head back to Chicago, Horatio kissed his family farewell for their boat journey across the oceans with plans to meet up with them in the days to come.

Back in Chicago with only nine days passed since seeing his family, Horatio received a telegram that simply stated, "Saved alone". The telegram was from his wife. The "Villa de Havre" the vessel on which Anna and their four daughters had set sail on towards England had collided with the English vessel, "The Lochearn". All four daughters were swept off the deck vanishing into the depths of the ocean. Anna herself was swept away but was saved by floating debris holding her nearly lifeless body up and being rescued by the search party.

I find it absolutely normal that Anna's first response was one of despair. I find it absurdly amazing that Anna's second response was one of thanksgiving to God for her many blessings. This was an automatic response just moments after the tragedy! Horatio, upon hearing the news traveled across the waves to meet his wife. During his journey the ship's captain graciously pointed out the spot of the recent tragedy. Horatio gazed upon the seas and then retreated to his cabin where he wrote the following words to, "It is Well with My Soul". As you read the verses think of how much Horatio suffered. Not many of us can say we've been through as much. Draw strength from Horatio and apply it to whatever hurdle you face.

> *When peace, like a river, attendeth my way,*
> *When sorrows like sea billows roll;*
> *Whatever my lot, Thou has taught me to say,*
> *It is well, it is well, with my soul.*
>
> *It is well, with my soul,*
> *It is well, with my soul,*
> *It is well, it is well, with my soul.*
>
> *Though Satan should buffet, though trials should come,*
> *Let this blest assurance control,*
> *That Christ has regarded my helpless estate,*
> *And hath shed His own blood for my soul.*

It is well, with my soul,
It is well, with my soul,
It is well, it is well, with my soul.

My sin, oh, the bliss of this glorious thought!
My sin, not in part but the whole,
Is nailed to the cross, and I bear it no more,
Praise the Lord, praise the Lord, O my soul!

It is well, with my soul,
It is well, with my soul,
It is well, it is well, with my soul.

And Lord, haste the day when my faith shall be sight,
The clouds be rolled back as a scroll;
The trump shall resound, and the Lord shall descend,
Even so, it is well with my soul.

It is well, with my soul,
It is well, with my soul,
It is well, it is well, with my soul.

I remember going to Grandma and Grandpa's house as a young child. As you walk into their house, to the right is a small three level bookcase. It's been there longer that I've been alive. The same "Little Sunshine" books have also been there. They've been read hundreds of times by me and my few cousins. I wonder how their pages are still intact. They look identical and brand new as they did when I was little. The pages aren't damaged or frayed. The colors aren't faded.

I passed my time at their house through the worlds opened by these books, a small array of old fashioned toys and my imagination led me with pencil and paper. There was also the backyard to explore where Grandpa's johnboat made its home. There was also silence. Lots of sitting still. Being quiet. Being scared. Obedience laced the air.

One of my most vivid memories of Grandma and Grandpa's house occurred when I was probably seven or eight. It was one of the rare occasions of spending the night at their house and I was having cereal for breakfast. It was a plain, no-taste, fiber enriched adult cereal. In order to eat the breakfast provided, which I was expected to do, my little fingers attached to my little hands reached for the sugar jar. I poured. And,

I poured. Then I took a bite and discovered I had just poured heaping tablespoons of salt all over my bowl of cereal. I sat in silence and I ate my entire bowl of salt drenched cereal. This is probably my most clear memory of their house and probably my first true taste of depression. A depressed person will rarely stand up for their own needs. Doing so would be a display of selfishness. If asked, a depressed person will always say they are "fine". No matter how deep in the trenches they fall, they will still be "fine".

I do remember some fun times as a kid at Grandpa's house. Bubba and I would waste away afternoons by playing ping pong on the front porch. No net or anything but we would play for hours on the concrete front porch just hitting the ball back and forth to each other. I'd rather be outside exploring the world when at their house. Inside meant being quiet, sitting up straight and not touching anything. It was a place I escaped inside my head and through my imagination. I could be a pretty quiet kid and there were old fashioned toys such as tinker toys and spinning tops that would catch my eye. There was an abundance of paper and pencils and I would draw the days away.

Two boys lived across the street. They were about the same age as Bubba and me. We played whiffle ball and video games with them. We also went on walks up and down the small house-lined street full of memories from my mother's childhood. We would play in the backyard, home to Grandpa's fishing boat. We would imagine adventures on the water. Even with these distractions it was as if you were walking on glass with Grandpa. I was always afraid the floor which I walked upon was going to crack and crumble beneath my feet.

There were times when the house was filled with laughter and chatter that camouflaged the collapsing floor beneath our feet. Some of my best memories at Grandpa's were fish fries and family card games of Rook. We often ate Sunday lunch there, driving over after church. Always, a fish fry. Grandma always cooked the fries in the same oil as she had cooked the fish. It gave them a grainy crunchy texture, but they were delicious. I usually got to sit at the end, between the table and the window because you had to slither in the tight space to fit. The rest of the chairs were filled with my mom's siblings and their spouses. I don't remember doing anything on those Sunday's except for eating!

The fish we ate were from Grandpa's catch the day before. That's how Bubba (my childhood name for my brother) got to know Grandpa, unlike few others did. Grandpa would take him fishing. Bubba never really talked about those expeditions, those memories captured while spending hours upon calm lake waters in the limiting space of the small boat. But, they definitely bonded on those waters. He grew to respect Grandpa. They shared a love for fishing and the outdoors and he connected to Grandpa like few others. I've never understood it and Bubba has never talked about those rare and special experiences.

To this day Bubba doesn't talk about Grandpa killing himself. Bubba never seemed to be angry like the rest of us. I don't understand really anything about Grandpa. Not his life or his death or his relationship with Bubba. Maybe the two of them are too much alike. Maybe Grandpa was too close to Bubba's own heart and his own weaknesses. I don't know. What I do know, is deep down, I'm jealous of the relationship they had. Grandpa never showed any interest in me. At lengths he didn't talk to me at all.

Grandpa spent a lot of time fishing. It was really a passion of his and I believe it was also an escape from the toils of human interaction. Those of us in the family with depression all like seclusion and this was one way for him to get away. His other escape was his occupation. He was a truck driver so he spent hours on the road by himself. That's definitely a thread of depression connecting the men in our family. They tend to choose jobs where they spend a lot of time away from other people. They choose to hibernate away and alone from others. Grandpa worked hard as a truck driver, being the consonant provider for his family. We might be depressed but we disguise ourselves in our hard work.

Depression has a great reach and affects everyone even if you don't personally suffer from it. My relationship with Grandma suffers from it. I'll take the blame for the strain but I could never understand why she stood up for Grandpa, through his suicide, the funeral and ever since. To me her actions and her words validated his suicide. Justified how he treated people and made them feel unloved and unwanted. Maybe it's a generational thing and as a wife she was showing respect for her husband but to me it's just a lack of being honest about the real situation. Grandpa was depressed. And his isolation, his anger and his temperament were a result of his depression. If we can't admit these simple connections then the thread and impact gets longer and stronger.

Grandpa's suicide is a looming shadow of guilt and mystery over the family tree. Its reach is spreading into new generations, making imprints on the young and the old. The emotions surrounding Grandpa's suicide go to all extremes. Guilt, doubt, fear, anger and unresolved questions follow us like an umbrella overhead and a shadow at our feet. Has forgiveness and acceptance taken place? Probably not. Has an understanding soothed the wounds? Some, maybe. We are all survivors dealing with the cold truth of a dead grandpa and the chilling effects of the genetic strains of depression running through our own veins that seem to dull our appetite for life.

3) Getting Rid Of Dead Weight

What does a depressed person look like? A depressed person can look like you; can look like me. A person with depression can be highly functional. Most would be shocked to discover the depressed amongst them. To me depression is a weight that drags me downward creating effort in everything. Little things become hard and your body goes into protective mode urging you into isolation, drowning you of your last ounce of energy. Normal anxiety transforms into anger forming a shield around true emotions. Agitation becomes rage. Tiredness becomes exhaustion. Challenges become burdens. Little steps become huge weights dragging you inward and downward.

You do not have to be depressed to feel weighed down. What is weighing you down? Is there a grudge you've held on to? Is there a habit you need to break? Is there a friend you just can't let go of even though they aren't a good influence on you and don't have your best interest at heart? Are you depressed?

We all have memories, people and things in our life that are weighing us down. We need to correct them if possible and other times we just need to break the ties that bind. If we are weighed down by negative Earthly things then we aren't allowing God to do everything He has planned for us. In admitting these grudges and negative thoughts in our lives it allows God to help us turn the negative into a positive. What is your needless weight?

One of my weights has been my relationship with my Grandma. It has been patchy for several years.

It wasn't great before Grandpa committed suicide and I've struggled even more since the day he committed suicide. I could never come to grips with some of the reactions and statements my grandmother made at the time. Obviously, dealing with a suicide is a very complicated multi-layered situation and can be scrutinized from a multitude of angles. From my perspective, Grandma loved Grandpa and maybe that love caused her to overlook the reality of his actions. My belief about this built a distance between me and Grandma. Gradually the valleys between us grew into canyons.

Just recently I decided that the canyon was continuing to get deeper and it needed to stop. It didn't really matter who was right or who was wrong. It was my responsibility to bring peace to the relationship with my Grandma. It wasn't her issue. In fact, she might not have even known there was an issue. However, it is very clear what the Lord says. He says we should let go of our grievances. "*Let all bitterness and wrath and anger and clamor and slander be put away from you, along with all malice. Be kind to one another, tenderhearted, forgiving one another, as God in*

Christ forgave you," Ephesians 4:31-32 ESV.

One of Grandpa's best tools to hide from his depression was to build a fortress around his heart and mind with cruel and angry words. Angry words from the depressed cause no harm to the speaker. The words cause comfort and protection. But to the person on the receiving end it is the exact opposite. The words cut to the heart. You feel like you are dodging bullets of cruel words and demeaning phrases. You have no way to dodge them or to fight back. At the same time the depressed person doesn't care and when somebody truly doesn't care then there is nothing to be done to change it.

The words of the depressed person are usually targeted straight at the people they love the most. The words usually fall on the ears of family and friends, the ones they love the most.

I, like many was the target of Grandpa's malicious words. The exact words or subject matter are not important. The words were harsh. They left a dent in my heart. And, they led to Grandpa choosing not to say any words to me. No words from my Grandpa's mouth were directed at me for the last three years of his life.

The words and then lack thereof were painful, intimate and merciless. Then, I was angry at Grandpa for his suicide and his inability to close our wound prior to his act. I've carried around hurt feelings ever since because I always felt Grandma supported him and never admitted his wrongs both before and after the suicide. Grandma said few words about either incident to me. She neither stood up agreeing with Grandpa nor did she deviate from his words. After Grandpa's suicide she told me that Grandpa had wished the best for me and wanted to be a part of my life. I felt like this was a lie slapping me in the face leaving a permanent welt between me and Grandma.

Before I continue you must know that my grandma is a wonderful woman. She is the mother of five. She has devoted her life to her family and the church. Yes, we've had some bumps along the way but haven't we all? She's had to deal with a lot of curve balls in her life and I know she has based all of her decisions on what she thought was right and what she thought God wanted her to do. She is a strong woman and though I might not agree with some of her choices I respect her and love her deeply. And, I know the feelings are reciprocated.

Obviously, there is a lot to this situation and now isn't the time to go into its depths and analyze it from all the angles. The purpose of this part of the story is my relationship with Grandma and how Grandpa's depression effected it. In addition to my feelings about her action or inaction, I know I misdirected my anger and hurt at Grandpa to her because simply stated; Grandpa took himself out of the equation.

Why am I writing about this? It isn't because it comes easy. Obviously, this has very much made an imprint on my heart and soul. It's also proof that it's never too late to say you're sorry. In many ways I've always felt Grandma owed me an apology. But, when it comes down to it does it really matter?

I mentally approached my conversation with Grandma with only one goal in mind: to say I WAS

SORRY for MY part. I had absolutely no expectations of a reciprocal apology. I had no intention of hashing out the details. It would have brought no good to either of us. My sole purpose was to say I was sorry. And, I'm glad I did.

The weight was lifted. I carry a lighter load. Are all the bad feelings erased? Not completely. I am far from perfect. But, I can say that I'm truly sorry for holding on for so long. I still have a long way to go. Maybe, one day, on the other side, I can talk face to face with Grandpa and come to a better understanding of his words and actions. Maybe not. But, for now I can walk forward. I've opened the door to a new chapter with my Grandma. I've let go of the callous feelings I held. They were doing no good. They were only hurting me and weighing me down. Now I am free from them.

I encourage you to let go. Let go and let a little more light shine within your heart for all to see. "*Be kind to one another, tenderhearted, forgiving one another as God forgave you,*" Ephesians 4:32 RSV. The guilt I grasped certainly did not help my own situation. It was a tumor just like my depression. The negativity in my heart left no room for God's light and left a door open for depression to pass through.

Complete dread might come close to describing my anticipation about my conversation with my grandmother. It was beyond uncomfortable. It was hard to admit my faults. And, it was hard to accept her lack of ownership of the issues. What's the best we can do when we don't know how to handle something? Ask for help!

Ask God for help! He wants us to find strength in Him. It is not a weakness to ask for help! I envy people who easily ask for help because I am horrible at it. When something isn't going right it is my nature to try and figure it out all by myself. Many times I waste precious time going in circles when a friend could have quickly given me a solution. Not only is it ignorant to waste so much time that is a gift from God but when you really think about it, it's also very selfish. If you think you can do it all by yourself or better than anyone else you must think pretty highly of yourself! By asking others for help you are allowing them the opportunity to show the gifts and strengths God has given them. And, you're giving each other the chance to grow and learn!

Even more than asking for our brother and sister's help God wants us to lean on Him for help! Sometimes I take for granted that God already knows my thoughts so I fail to actually communicate them. But we need to talk with Him. We need to lay down our thoughts, our anxieties, our needs and our thanks to Him on a continual basis. It's a key ingredient to developing an authentic relationship with Him and it's the only true way to release our fears and our sadness. If you give your burdens to God on a daily basis and ask for His grace and mercy then He will give it to you! But, you have to put the plan in action. You have to ask for His help! You have to open the door to receive His promises and His light.

Do you receive God's unending and abundant promises? Are you not for sure? Could you not be reaching your happiness potential because you're not receiving His blessings? Think of what your life could be like if your heart was completely open to receiving all of

His promises. This must be THE secret to living a happy Earthly life! If you take away only one thing from this book let it be this: In order to really be happy you must be receiving God's promises.

Feel overwhelmed in your life? Too many things on your to do list? Too many responsibilities? Too many places to be at one time? STOP! Stop. Be Quiet. Listen. Ask God to show you what is truly important. Reorganize your life. Simplify. If something is truly worrying you and weighing you down then try this equation:

Prayer + Faith + Action = A Happy & Balanced Life

It's that simple. Pray about your concern. Have faith that God will take care of you. Then act on that Faith. You will be eternally happy.

Yesterday is gone and it is never coming back. No matter if it was good. No matter if it was bad. It is gone. Letting go of past grievances and hurt can be a very hard thing to do. Yet, that is what God does for us every second of the day. If you believe in Him and have a relationship with Him then He always forgives and lets you start anew. Release the weights from your past that are holding you back from your potential.

So if you've done something that causes you guilt let go of it because He has already forgotten. If someone else has done wrong to you let go of it because that is what God would do. It's not easy. We all struggle. But letting go is much better than carrying all the negative weight around.

4) The Other Side Of The Family Tree

I do not really have a full memory of Grandpa, my dad's father. I was only in second grade when he died. My memories are often reconstructed from stories I've heard, my own childhood experiences and smells, and photo albums. In order to enter into Grandpa and Grandma's world you had to maneuver through a maze of fragrant irises. There were so many they created a rainbow of God's color palette and you could smell them from around the corner. Every time I see an iris I think of Grandma.

Upon passing the house's threshold you would be hit with the Earthly smell of moth balls! You would also see just slightly to the left, Grandpa in his overalls sitting in his well-worn chair. Grandpa's tall, lean body filled the entire seat and his knobby knees trying to escape his overalls created a barrier from entry. Sitting on his knobby knees is my main memory of Grandpa. That and being at his funeral. Those two photographic memories live in my mind and are the totality of the details I retain of Grandpa.

Grandpa and Grandma had the largest garden I'd ever seen. Walking up and down the paths, the cornstalks brushing against my arms and towering over my head led me into a world of imagination. Did I love Grandma's corn? Oh, yes. And, I still love corn on the cob to this day. I always felt so tiny within the shade of the cornstalks! My brother and I both picked up the love of gardening from our grandparents. We've yet to master the art of growing Grandma's monstrous and juicy tomatoes! My tomatoes have yet to taste quite as good.

There were two cherry trees rooted behind their

house. My brother and I were charged with cherry picking. We would sit in opposing trees for hours and the day would end with us both having sour stomachs because we had our routine down. Eat two cherries. Put one in the bucket. Eat two cherries. Put one in the bucket. At that pace it took all day to complete the chore. But, at the end of the day the cherries were magically transformed into Grandma's famous and delicious cherry cream pie. It's funny how so many of my memories at their house center on food. Sadly, one of those trees is the same place Grandpa chose to end his life.

While at their house if I wasn't in the garden, I was either in the backyard or on a bike riding on the cracked sidewalks around their block and through the cemetery down the street.

The backyard wasn't big but there were plants and sheds and the garden to explore. I spent hours looking at the rustic and worn tools, the garden hoses and other gadgets stored in the sheds. Most of all I remember having fun with my brother. Playing hide and seek and tag. And, just taking it all in; only the way an innocent young child can do.

I loved riding my bike around the block. Freedom blowing through my hair. I was easily entertained by counting all of the cracks. Going crazy fast and then lazy slow. I also explored the cemetery. It had great paths. Weird, how I never thought about all the dead people there, the bodies I was amongst. Again, the innocence of a child is precious. Now, I look back and I see the irony. The innocent child bike riding through the cemetery where her suicidal grandpa was buried. However, these are good memories. I smile thinking back.

I have many more memories of Grandma. She lived to age 92. She was a strong, opinionated woman. A matriarch of her day. I have few memories of Grandpa. I remember him sitting in his chair. I remember his overalls. I remember his Sunday hat, one reminiscent of an old movie. I have both of their hats. Grandpa's velvety black handsome hat and grandma's garden, sun shading hat. They both bring me joy and grief when I look at them.

The realization of my paternal Grandpa's suicide did not become my reality until Grandpa committed the same gruesome act. I remember my paternal Grandpa being sick. My most vivid memory of this time was him being hospitalized. For some reason I thought he had cancer. I don't really think anyone told me that but for some reason that's what I thought. I knew he was sick. He recovered enough to return home. I really don't remember much after he went home. I don't know how long he was at home after that hospital stay before he committed suicide. I remember the phone ringing one day and then he was dead. Even as an adult I still thought he had died of natural causes. However, only a couple days after Grandpa killed himself I was shocked to discover that my other Grandpa had as well.

One could determine that my Grandfathers suffered from two different kinds of depression. Grandpa struggled with depression throughout his life. It intertwined his thoughts and his actions on a daily basis and for many years. On the other hand I believe my paternal Grandpa was faced with a single situation pushing him into depression. His body and mind were being taken over by an illness and he was unable to live the life he was accustomed to living. He decided he didn't want to live anymore because he didn't have control. It was easier to end his life than to proceed. Even though their experiences were different the results were the same.

Grandpa's source of finalization was a rope. My paternal Grandpa's was also a rope. He chose to hang himself in one of the cherry trees that held the imagination of me and my brother. Innocence turned dreadful in a split second.

In an instant both of my grandfathers changed the course of their family's lives. According to www.wikihow.com an instant is how quickly death can occur in a hanging. There are several factors that dictate how long it takes for death to occur, if it happens at all. The main factors include the person's weight and the distance they fall. The fall leads to death by decapitation, a broken neck or suffocation. Hanging doesn't always produce death. Many recover from a hanging however, they along with their family may have to deal with the person being paralyzed for life or spinal cord injuries that lead to death over many years or a few days.

Six simple steps created their weapon of choice. The assembly took only a few minutes. You can even look it up on the World Wide Web (www.wikihow.com).

1. Start with a piece of rope about 3 feet long.
2. Get one end and fold it into three's (remember to have some rope left at the end).
3. Now with the string left at the end slowly wind it round the third (it should now look a bit like a hangman's noose)
4. When you are finished there should be a loop at both ends.
5. With the string which has been wound round the thirds, put it through the loop at the end.
6. Now once the loop is fully tightened, it should be ready to be used (it should have one giant loop at one end and a piece of string at the other end).

Simple instructions. Six steps. A few minutes. An instant. Both of my grandpas are gone. Our lives changed forever.

I remember Grandpa's funeral through the eyes of an eight year old. It was probably the first funeral I had attended. It is the first funeral I remember. Sitting on the side with family members separated from the other mourners seemed weird to me. I didn't understand why we were sectioned off from everyone else. It seemed like the funeral went on for days in a dead silence. You could have heard a pin drop in that small-town funeral home

I remember being at the cemetery; the same one where I had ridden my bike so many miles. I really only have snapshots stuck in my mind. I remember sitting on my Aunt's lap back at Grandpa's house after the burial ceremony. Listening to relatives say everything was okay. Nothing was really okay. In many ways it's still not okay today.

Today I deal with the repercussions of suicide and depression on both sides of the family tree. It must be a very small percentage of the Earth's population whom can claim to be in that category. My brother and I didn't have a great chance of escaping the wrath of depression. It was throwing darts at us from all directions determined to take root in its target.

It's so hard to comprehend how two men (both grandfathers) of such stern religious beliefs left their families behind. Suicide seems to be the ultimate act of selfishness. I believe it is not possible for those dealing with the repercussions of suicide to understand the victim's torment or to experience peace without the loving hand of God. It's one of those things you must give to God to hold for you. You can go crazy trying to figure it out, trying to rationalize it. You can become overwhelmed with grief and anger. You have to give it to God. *"Trust in the Lord with all your heart; do not depend on your own understanding. Seek his will in all you do, and he will show you which path to take,"* Proverbs 3:5-6 NLT.

5) My Own World Of Solitude

Most who know me would be surprised to hear me describe myself as an introvert. Deep inside my soul is where I seek to find solitude. I lose myself in a book, in quiet spaces, and having "alone" time is a must or my life wavers out of balance. These inner traits of my personality served as the perfect camouflage for my depression. My friends and co-workers would never know it because from the outside looking in, I'm actually quite outgoing and active.

I've always been a leader at work and at school. I have no problems with speaking in front of a crowd. However, I think I'm much more anxious than other people when placed in social situations. I'm very concerned with the outcomes of my actions. I don't tend to worry about what people think about me but I always want to do my best and it causes me much stress. According to Richard Winter in his book "When Life Goes Dark" many depressed people incorporate one of four of the following thought patterns in their daily routine and logic.

1. If I'm not accepted by others I can't be happy.

2. Mistakes aren't allowed.

3. If you disagree with me you don't like me.

4. My value as a person is dependent upon what you think of me.[1]

I find this concept to probably be accurate however it is also interesting because they all focus on others and depression is such a personal disease. I decided early on, as far back as elementary school to not care about what others think of me. This shield was probably my first piece of protective armor. However, I recently discovered during a counseling session that even though I might not care what you think of me it makes me feel like I'm being selfish if I don't agree with what another person wants. Interesting!

Here's a typical scenario for me. Everyone is outside having fun. People are laughing and talking about the day as normal people do. Where am I? I'm inside curled up on the couch under a blanket. I'm alone and I feel at peace. If I was out there I would be fidgeting. My skin would be crawling and no one would know it but me. I appear normal on the outside. No one knows I would rather be alone. Looking back I think I was even like this as a kid. I really didn't have trouble playing alone. But, on the other hand, I had friends, just not many close friends. I still don't. I've never been shy. I just thought it was part of my personality, my make-up. And, I guess that is true. I just didn't know it was a defect. One so close to pushing me over the edge. I just wanted the pain to go away and to be at peace. I just wanted to be alone.

There is a constant voice, strong yet gentle, inside of me yearning to simply be alone. Relaxation is work. Socializing is work. I wish I could take my insides and shake them loose the way a swimmer or runner shakes their muscles and limbs readying themselves for an impending race. Having fun without a purpose isn't an option for me. It causes stress and anxiety to consume both my body and mind.

I find myself jealous of socially apt people. There are certain people who just make it all look easy. Some people just crave social interaction and it comes very natural. They can move in and out of conversations with ease. Words slip easily off their tongues and people gravitate to them. I can play the role. However, that is all it is. It's acting. It takes energy, effort and focus. It can be a mountain high load of work for an ant hill amount of fun.

I'm very good at hiding my insecurities, yet I often find myself hoping that I can escape into the solitude of my home. The act of escaping creates a sense of relief that envelopes my body. One could even say the feeling is addictive.

Sometimes I feel alone even when I'm in a room crowded with people. Do you ever feel alone? I'm physically in that room but I'm floating in my own hemisphere within my head. I know God doesn't want us to be alone and you never have to be lonely if you accept Him. By accepting Him He will constantly be with you and He will be within you. When you do feel lonely reach out to Him because He has promised that He will be there for you! *"He will never leave you. He will never forsake you,"* Hebrews 13:5 NIV. I know this urge to be alone holds me back from being the person God created me to be. It detracts from my ability to bear fruit for Him.

God also wants you to find comfort through relationships with friends, especially other believers because He knows that you will draw support and strength from them. He wants you to reciprocate by giving strength and support to others. *"Two are better than one, because they have better return for their labor: If one of them falls down, one can help the other up. But pity anyone who falls and has no one to help them up,"* Ecclesiastics 4:9-10 TNIV.

So accept the Lord. Surround yourself with friends and believers. And, if you still find yourself alone take comfort that He is there for you. Walk with God and you will never walk alone again.

I had the unique experience of living on a boat for nearly a year. Don't get me wrong, I wasn't roughing it. The boat was a 70-foot houseboat with two baths, four bedrooms and a full kitchen and living room. The dock had seven boats on both sides and my boat was at the end accompanied by a beautiful lake view. Other than living on a boat life was normal. I was there alone a lot of the time. I got up walked the dogs, went to work, came home, walked the dogs again, fixed supper and went to bed. Weekends were full of friends, boat rides and food. There would usually be about ten of us who would have dinner together each night either grilling on the boats or going to a local eatery.

In many ways it was a great adventure and many would be jealous of this lifestyle. My life had been simplified. Things had been eliminated. This I would recommend to anyone! It can be so freeing. On the other side, this was a time of realization, self- discovery and sometimes darkness for me. I never voiced my feelings to anyone but I slowly withdrew into myself, in the safe haven and solitude of the boat and my mind. I didn't even know it was happening at the time but looking back it was very obvious that this recipe of solitude, winter darkness and silence was a brewing combination to discover my own depression.

During the summer, especially on the weekends, the boat dock was a lively place. A very happy and social place. It could be a lot of fun, but for me it was exhausting. I would find myself withdrawing. Being around people, even if they were people I liked and loved wore on my nerves. I could always find relief when I retreated inside the boat. Alone. When Sunday night rolled around I would find my soul relaxing because people were departing to their homes and the dock would become quiet again. The isolation of the empty space was like slipping into a hot bath, escaping from all the pressures.

Is seclusion inherently a bad thing? No. Does being alone mean being depressed? No. Is the desire to be alone a selfish act? No. Though for me I have to always have my watchtower on high alert. I can't allow myself to slide down the slippery slope of solitude into a depressed stage. I must always seek balance. Solitude can be a blessing. Jesus gave us many examples. If Jesus found strength in times of solitude then it is highly likely we were made to do the same. Always maintain your equilibrium and draw strength from these examples:

"Very early in the morning, while it was still dark, Jesus got up, left the house and went off to a solitary place, where he prayed," Mark 1:35 NIV.

"And immediately He made His disciples get into the boat and go ahead of Him to the other side to Bethsaida, while He Himself was sending the multitude away. And after bidding them farewell, he departed to the mountain to pray," Mark 6:45-46 NASB.

"And they came to a place called Gethsemane; and He said to His disciples, "Sit here until I have prayed." And He took with Him Peter and James and John, and began to be very distressed and

troubled. And He said to them, "My soul is deeply grieved to the
point of death; remain here and keep watch." And He went a
little beyond them, and fell to the ground, and began praying,"
Mark 14:32-34 NAS.

"And when day came, He departed to a lonely place; and the
multitudes were searching for Him, and came to Him, and tried to
keep Him from going away from them," Luke 4:42 NASB.

"But He Himself would often slip away to the wilderness and
pray," Luke 5:16 NASB.

"In these days he went out to the mountain to pray, and all night
he continued in prayer to God," Luke 6:12 ESV.

     I've never pictured God as being gentle or quiet
but I think I was wrong. He is our Father. He is the
Counselor and Prince of Peace. I am drawn back to 1
Kings 10:1-18 where God comforted Elijah during his
time of depression and it really strikes a note in me.
God, through an angel gently touched Elijah, then told
him of the future plans He had for him. It is a moment
of consolation and compassion that God shared with
Elijah, one of empathy. Imagine the next time you are in

the trenches, God's hand gently resting on your shoulder and Him whispering in your ear that all is okay and that He is there to guide you. Find solitude in the Lord, not by simply escaping.

No matter what your struggle, study Elijah to find encouragement. In Kings 19 you'll find Elijah's emotions plummet from the highest high to the lowest low. Elijah had been busy doing God's work, battle after battle and he was exhausted. Under God's guidance he had succeeded. He thought it was over and relief was finally his but he was wrong.

Just when he thought it was over he now faced the wrath of being hunted by Jezebel! What did Elijah do? He mustered up every ounce of energy he could and he ran, and ran and ran. One can conjure up images of Forest Gump running! Elijah traveled over 400 miles in 40 grueling days and nights through the sweltering desert till he collapsed at Mount Horeb! Have you ever worked that hard to escape pressure? You just can't take it anymore. Talk about the fight or flight scenario! Elijah cried to God, "I've had enough.....take my life, I'm alone, get me out of here, I've been busy working for you and look at where it's gotten me!"

How would you describe Elijah? These are some of the words that come to my mind….exhausted, despair, betrayed, depressed, useless, failure, afraid, angry and bitter to name a few.

We've all found ourselves feeling these things at some point. Things don't go as planned, we face failure, we face internal disappointments and we are disappointed and hurt by others. Elijah experienced this emotional rollercoaster all at one time. He was not only depressed and exhausted, he was angry at God. Elijah longed for answers and explanations. He also longed for the comfort of God's arms and His presence. He needed assurance that after all he'd been through God was still there and he was going to be okay.

But wasn't Elijah limiting his faith in God? Wasn't his anger towards God a sin? He had given up on himself and on God. God had always delivered him to triumph so why would he doubt now?

When he finally stopped running, collapsing from his internal and limited resources he cried out to God. How did God respond? Did God yell in frustration and disappointment at Elijah's lacking faith? No, God comforted Elijah. He was gentle and encouraging, urging Elijah to get up and retreat from his solitude and get back to "the real world."

You see solitude can be a great tool for reflection, growth, insight and more but God didn't make us to be alone. You can't live in a one person world and fully receive God's love. When I pull away from the world, hungering for a secluded retreat I must proceed with caution or my depression will find strength and quietly but slowly take over. It will spread like a cancer. The older I've become the more I've withdrawn to my own carved out haven. I've become better at creating excuses to get out of social settings, to leave the party early, to flee. It's as if you don't even realize it's happening, but overtime my life has transformed, yet the people surrounding me have no idea. I've recoiled into myself yet no one even seems to have noticed.

For some, depression seeps into their system like the drip of an IV. It's slow and steady. In fact you might not even feel it. With each drip, the depressed soul retreats further within. The outside world drifts a little farther away. Activities become dull. Limitations are the norm and stimulation subsides.

The Lord created a competitive spirit within me. More competitive than most, striving to my limits in order to avoid the taste of loss. I've always been a leader on a gym floor, very competitive. I'm depressed but my competitive drive serves as a façade, like a chameleon. I fade into the world around me while falling into my own inner refuge. My brother, my uncle, and other family members are burdened with their own realities of depression and they also withdraw. They are also extremely competitive yet they choose occupations that provide them escapes. It was easy for me to see depression in their worlds yet I was completely blind to my own.

I play a game of volleyball with the team but as soon as the last point is played I quickly bolt from the scene. I find myself looking forward to dinners out and parties with friends, but then the date comes and I would rather back out of these engagements. I get there and I have fun but eventually my skin starts to crawl. My shoes begin to swallow my feet. I can feel all my nerve endings and I can't sit still. My leg starts to shake, back and forth. These annoying panicky feelings don't go away until I've weaseled away to the comfort of my home. To the paradise of my own bed. To my dogs comforting me. I throw off my shoes and rid my toes of my socks. Freedom. I sink into my bed and instantly the weight begins to lift off my chest and the bugs crawling over my skin begin their departure. I sigh a long breath of relief and begin to relax.

These motions, even routines have cemented into my life over the years. It's weird because even with my family's history, my view of depression was severely skewed. Depression has such a stigma. People envision someone who hasn't brushed their hair in a week, not going to work and sleeping on the couch while eating potato chips during intermission. While some people of course do experience these, it's not my reality. I experienced a very slow metamorphous. I went from being highly, even overly active and motivated to doing just enough to get by.

I've discovered that I have to have balance within my own personality! It's kind of a weird concept! I like being by myself. I like snuggling down with just me and a good book. There is absolutely nothing wrong with this! I have to repeatedly tell myself that this is not a selfish act. And, I can't let depression take this joy away from me. On the other hand, I can't let depression completely take away the joys of relationships and social gatherings. I have to work to have balance. Through God's aid I can take steps to achieve the needed balance.

If I focus on Him everything else has a way of falling into place. God only asks you to take little steps towards Him. Each day take a little step closer to God. Say a prayer. Say thanks. Forgive someone. Help someone. Have a little faith - as small as a mustard seed. Read the Bible for a few minutes. What will you receive for your little steps? You will discover your equilibrium. You will receive His grace. All of it. All of God's grace!

Have a plan but make sure it is God's plan. When you follow your own routine, wave after wave, sometimes the water can drift you in the wrong direction. As you plan for balance make sure your foundation is your relationship with God. If not, you are likely to fall off course. Focusing on what God has planned for you is like having a built-in GPS system.

How do you know what God wants for you? How do you know what plans He has to restore happiness in your life? How do you know if you are receiving His promises for you? You have to begin with coming to know God and developing a relationship with Him. God has given us the ultimate tool for knowing Him, the Bible. In order for you to know what God has planned for you, you must first know Him. Reading the Bible can seem like a daunting task for many but please do not get overwhelmed. Give yourself an attainable goal like to read three chapters a day. Try out different Bible translations and pick the one that responds to you. A great way to go through the Bible is with a devotional type Bible that leads you through daily lessons on a journey through the Bible. Start by giving it five minutes a day. No matter how busy you are I guarantee you can find five minutes!

A transformation will start happening in your heart. Negative thoughts will turn to positive ones. As you read, seek out the promises God has given to you and write them on your heart. Write them in a journal and review them. This process will give you strength, hope and comfort. *"I can do everything through him who gives me strength,"* Philippians 4:13 NIV.

As you search, observe how God treats and directs those who are burdened. Carry those examples in your heart the next time you are feeling down and then pray. You will find that God is a loving Father. He is not judgmental. He is compassionate. Take this comfort with you on your daily journey. *"The Lord is close to the brokenhearted and saves those who are crushed in spirit,"* Psalm 34:18 NIV.

You will actually start to travel through life making decisions on what you think God's plan is for you. You will take the focus off of you and onto God! You will look at others as you think God would look at them. You will build trust and dependence on God to lead you.

Isn't depression the same as tunneled vision where everything is seen through the lens of self? It's time for a vision check. Take off your glasses and put on God's! Let your guard crumble and your strength come from the Lord. Take in a deep breath of relief. You can be yourself!

Before you close your eyes tonight pray that tomorrow will be an authentic day in which God leads you down His chosen path. Pray that the road He has put you on is blessed and full of opportunities to touch others. Pray for the confidence to fully share your weaknesses and struggles with others so you might grow and help others along the way. Pray this tomorrow and the next day and the next. Remember that no matter what, it is grace that saves you.

Admit it to yourself right now that you will make mistakes. God has given us the tools we need to maneuver through mistakes. He gave us the Bible to learn from and to be able to grow closer to Him. He gave us prayer to communicate our needs and our thanksgivings to Him. He gave us faith, hope and grace so we can have the courage to get up when we fall and move forward. Remember that you are made in the image of God and your litmus test is not one of Earthly perfection because in God's eyes you are already perfect! Through the crucifixion of Jesus you were promised forgiveness, mercy and endless love. All of these promises were made with your unique self in mind! *"In him and through faith in him we may approach God with freedom and confidence,"* Ephesians 3:12 NIV.

Do you ever feel weak? Do you ever feel afraid? Do you ever feel as if you have no control? We all experience these emotions because of struggles we endeavor or even just because we feel insecure. Maybe you've detoured from the path God built for you. However, these emotions are all unnecessary because God has given us the ultimate freedom and power to approach Him about anything and everything. Do not become overwhelmed or caught in a web of guilt, sadness and self-pity.

I believe God made salvation a very simple process for each of us to achieve. As humans we tend to over-complicate things and get caught up in all the details. I'm not saying that the details aren't important. They are important and we should study, discuss and have healthy debates. However, when it comes down to it God made it simple for us.

- He wants us to be with Him.
- He sent His son to die on the cross so we can be with Him.
- We have the simple choice to believe, confess and choose to accept his forgiveness and salvation.
- He's given us a way to get to know Him: the Bible.
- He's given us a way to communicate with Him: prayer.

He's given us the ability to choose these things and we can communicate with Him in confidence knowing that He will hear every word and answer every prayer. No matter how small or big the request. Choose not to make it complicated. Choose God. Choose to keep it simple.

6) Coming To Terms With My Own "D"

We all have different struggles we deal with on a daily and regular basis. One of my struggles is depression. Most of my friends and co-workers would never know this. In fact, most would be surprised to hear this. Do I mope around being sad? No, that's not it. Depression rears its head in my life in the way of seclusion and irritability. This might not sound too life altering but coming from a family where depression is genetic and depression has led to multiple suicides it's a struggle I take very seriously.

It's something I pray about. I pray for wisdom in how to deal with it. I pray that the symptoms lessen overtime. I pray that it doesn't affect those around me. What do you struggle with? Big and small? Do you pray about your struggles? If not, start today. Do you have true friends you can confide in and lean on? If not, seek them out.

No matter what your personal struggles, remember that God is at your side waiting for you to reach your hand out to Him so He can help you!

One of the hardest changes and transformations I've personally encountered on my journey to live with and conquer my depression is to be truly authentic and honest with myself and those I love. Admitting my wrongs and my mistakes have been hard lessons learned. Claiming the responsibility of my actions or sometimes inactions caused by simply not being me and afraid of showing my true inner self to others has been heart wrenching at times. I've caused hurt within my soul and to those I love the most. Part of my journey to come to grips with my depression brought the realization that I hadn't truly embraced the real me. For many reasons I wasn't being the person God intended me to be. Depression is part of the reason. It has the power to hide in deep dark places and cover up reality.

Discovery of my own depression didn't become a realization until I had to take a closer examination of another person's reality with depression. I guess it's kind of like the phenomenon of being a professional landscaper, yet your own front yard is unkempt.

Depression was swarming all around me yet I couldn't identify it within me! The dots were disconnected! I know now that it is not normal to fantasize about driving your car into oncoming traffic! It's insane to think that is normal but I did. Those thoughts entered my mind often.

I had known that my brother (Bubba) dealt with his own depression but it had never really affected me directly and I hadn't seen it for myself inside the walls of his family's home. As someone suffering from depression, I knew that you can get sucked into thinking everything is okay and that your depression only affects yourself. However, it is quite the opposite and at that time it was confronting him head on. His depression was affecting his family, the ones he loved and cared about the most.

Our depressions our similar in that depression makes us retreat and escape away from other people. That's really the center of my depression. I guess I'm lucky that I didn't receive the full front of the family curse. I don't get angry at people. That's the other family symptom. Don't get me wrong, I'm not talking angry in a physical way. But, anger exemplified by short and hurtful words. This is the central theme with our men and their depressions. However, if I was genuinely honest with myself I would admit that even though I rarely get angry depression rears its head from me in the form of irritability.

If you take a quick glimpse at depression, anger probably isn't the first word that comes to mind. However, anger is one of the most common symptoms or side effects of depression. If you take a thorough examination it makes sense. A while back there was a commercial where birds kept flying directly into windows crashing their beaks. They wanted to get through but couldn't see the glass. I think this is true of the depressed. It's certainly how I feel at times. I'm standing by myself on one side of the glass wall looking out to the world and I want to venture out into all it has to offer but when I finally summon the courage to move forward my face is flattened into the glass. I retreat until courage is found again. This scenario repeats until courage is replaced with resentment and agitation. The world sees a rude, angry person. The depressed sees a frustrated, exhausted soul crying for relief.

Seeing how depression was affecting my brother and the people he loved the most struck a chord with me. It was as if a mirror was shining back at my heart. So much so that I started with serious self-examination. I discovered what I really always knew, that I was also depressed and my depression had found its home in withdrawal and isolation. It had drained me of energy and had tied me to a very limited life. It had taken me away from fun. Even more, I had lost my true self.

When depression sets in I feel like I'm walking on a cloud. It's not a cheery floating on air feeling. It's a gray rainy cloud and it's as if I'm in this life but not really feeling any of it. You know how sometimes you are driving and you get to your destination but once you've arrived you don't remember the journey. That's what it's like but it's all the time. You are here with your feet planted on the ground but you have no real connection to anything or anyone. You are physically present but emotionally unattached. It doesn't have to be a constant sadness, at least not for me, it's just an unwillingness or desire to let myself care or put myself out there in the real world. It's going through the motions but on an entirely unapproachable level. It's controlling your environment so you avoid pain.

Irritability on steroids is how depression can present itself to me. When I'm in social situations the void can make my skin crawl like there are thousands of prickly points trying to escape from under my skin. I'll be at work, or in a restaurant or simply relaxing or lying in bed at night and my brain is concentrated on trying to escape from my clothes because I'm trapped and drowning inside of my body. I have the sensation of being held down by a tremendous weight. I try and focus on something soothing, a beach, a cool breeze on a warm day. It lets me relax for two seconds and then the sensation returns. My leg shakes uncontrollably under my desk at work. Every cell in me is trying to escape. The weight is immeasurable. Sometimes it rolls in like dominos. One situation starts a thought in your head that leads to another and so on. Your mind is now chaotic and your sense of control lost, leading to more depression.

It's not like that every day but it comes on when you sometimes least expect it. It might be when I'm alone or it might be when I'm in a crowd of people. Anxiety can bring it on. Stress can trigger it. Being alone or sad about something might do it. Or it might have been a great day and it comes and hits me upside the head that evening like a punching bag.

Sometimes my heart can pound so hard I'm sure it's going to fall out of my chest onto the floor and roll away. At other times I wonder if it's still inside me.

Depression can be a retreat, protecting me from the outside world, carving a space between me and the chance of getting hurt. A zone made just for me, a hideaway.

Before I leave from work I've made a mental list of tasks to achieve for the evening. The list can easily vanish by the time I hit the driveway at night. The simplest of activities become chores instead of accomplishments. Then nothing gets marked off the list and failure sets in again! I've learned that I can't procrastinate. I have to plan and I have to act. Some days are easier than others but being aware of the process creates a huge opportunity for future days of happiness.

For some stupid reason there is still a stigma about depression. Yes, I think it's stupid. It is proven that certain forms of depression are rooted in chemical imbalances and genetic code. Yes, I believe that in many cases medical treatment should be sought. And, I also believe that the Devil preys on depression like he does other diseases such as cancer, Alzheimer's and heart disease and uses them to encourage us to fall and to succumb to temptations and self-destruction.

Just as the Devil doesn't see the difference from affliction to affliction we shouldn't either. In all cases we should look to God's word to get us through, *"Come to Me, all ye who labor and heavy laden, and I will give you rest. Take My yoke upon you and learn from me, for I am gentle and lowly in heart, and you will find rest for your souls. For My yoke is easy and My burden is light,"* Matthew 11:28-30 NIV.

I finally decided it was time for me to take action. I surrendered and I made an appointment with the doctor. I was very nervous sitting in the doctor's waiting room. I had never been to this doctor before, yet alone being nervous about talking about my depression. Sitting in the waiting room, I wondered if I was in the wrong office because I was surrounded by a bunch of old people. It took forever. I wish I would have brought a book to read, something to distract the thoughts bouncing inside my head. And, touching magazines in a doc's office gives me the "heebie jeebies" just thinking about all the germs. I almost got up and left. My inner voice was on the verge of seducing me to leave.

By the time I was in an actual patient room my palms were sweating, my nerves were wrecked, and I just wanted to leave. It was worse than going to the gynecologist. The room was small, cold and had no windows. Why are doctor's offices always so cold? The doctor finally came in. She was actually a rather calming presence. Of course, she asked me why I was there. All I had to say was the word depression and tears started rushing down my face. I felt like a failure, as if I'd given up, given in. The tears wouldn't stop falling.

She asked me what made me think I was depressed. I started with both of my Grandpas committing suicide. Nothing like subtlety. I went further, explaining that I found myself withdrawing from social activities. The fact that I was beginning to crave isolation. I found motivation hard to come by and that wasn't normal for me. She asked if I thought of suicide. My response was no, I don't think about killing myself, but, I do think that if I were to die in a car accident or something similar it wouldn't be a big deal. It wouldn't be bad. I mean, heaven sounds like a grand place. I wouldn't want my family to suffer sadness but personally death has never sounded bad.

I walked away that day with a huge burden lifted off my heart and a prescription in my hand. Something about saying it out loud was a super release. The doctor was a supply of comfort and reassurance.

It took a couple days for me to start taking the medicine. I guess hesitation still halted my heart. It was quite expensive too so that didn't help. After a couple months, I began to notice small changes. I wasn't as fidgety in social settings, I was more relaxed overall. I wasn't as apprehensive about going places and doing things. I simply enjoyed life more.

After a few months, I stopped taking it. Doubt found me and I didn't think it was making a difference. Depression is deceitful and will convince you all is well. Probably similar to alcoholics convincing themselves that one drink will not hurt them. I soon got back on the medication.

I stayed on the meds for about a year and concluded again that I really didn't think they were having a big effect so I stopped taking them. When I did, it was as if I was going through withdrawal. My words were short and my anger was quick. I morphed into being like one of the guys in the family. As with all my family, the harsh words are usually heard the most by the ones we love the most. This led me to see a new doctor and get a new script. I've since worked with my doctor and we've adjusted the dosage and I'm doing much better. I can say I feel happy. I feel like myself. God has given me back me! I have the courage to be me. I had no idea how much of me I had lost. I can't go back in time to reclaim time lost but I can rely on God to lead me into the future as the person He intended me to be.

I am a proponent of medication under the guidance of a physician and/or psychiatrist for the treatment of depression. I've seen the devastating effects of depression in my own family. From multiple suicides and living lives of seclusion, depression can have detrimental effects on the depressed, their family, their work and their relationship with God. And, sometimes these effects are irreversible. I have personally experienced and witnessed relief medication can give. Why would God not want you to partake in modern medicine? Remember, that He is also a Physician. He is the ultimate Physician, so do not be led to believe that the pill is a magical pill. You must take an active role in controlling your mood and thoughts whether you are on medication or not.

Part of my "self-medication" was the process of writing down my experiences with depression. When I started studying and penning my family's journey it opened the door to joy. Writing has served as a sort of therapy for me. I've had to analyze my own good and bad parts. Self-inflection, if led by growth and change can be an energizing event. My blog was the ultimate turning point. It gave me goals and accountability. It gave me purpose. It took my focus off of me and onto others. It gave me excitement!

7) Goals, If Good, Can Be A Key To Happiness

I can easily succumb to the comforts depression provides me when I'm not focused on being healthy and happy. If you don't know where you are going or where you want to be you can end up anywhere feeling lost, alone and confused. You've probably heard those infamous words from a parent, coach or teacher before. I hate to say it but they were right on target.

If you have depression and don't have a plan on how to cope and not be depressed any more, then guess what road you've already chosen to travel? You've chosen to travel the road to more depression! As, Richard O'Connor, Ph.D. in his book "Undoing Depression" says one would not expect an alcoholic to simply say he's not going to drink anymore and poof he is suddenly cured! No, the alcoholic must also change his thought patterns, his habits, his activities, his entire life![2] And, believe me, this isn't easy. The same can be said of depression.

If you are unhappy with where you are in life. If you don't like your job. If your relationships are unhealthy. If there's anything you wish to change then this chapter applies to you.

Often my depression leaves me feeling empty, as if a big hole has replaced my heart. If I do not change my life and find ways to fill the hole then the depression dump truck backs in releasing more negative thoughts and creates a bigger hole. Scrutinize how you control your surroundings and how you spend your time. Look at who you choose to socialize with and all of your habits. Then make a plan on how to change the ones that make you vulnerable to depression or anything that's holding you down.

The best way to get where you want to go is to have a plan and that means having goals. This is one tactic that really helps me stay on the road to happiness. There are tons of articles and books out there about success and goals but we aren't talking about success. We're talking about being happy! The key though is to have good goals. I was fortunate to hear a very wise man speak about goals at a training seminar so don't think I'm the creator of this philosophy. However, the message from Randy Marshall (www.thepowerofpurpose.org) was so powerful that I had to share it.

What is a healthy goal? And, just how can a goal make you happy and help you deal with depression or other struggles? Most of modern society has an inaccurate and unhealthy definition of a good goal and this misconception leads to perceived failure. Now, some of the attributes of our preconceived notion of a good goal are absolutely great. For example, a goal should be simply stated. A goal should be measurable.

And, a goal should have a deadline. These are great guidelines, yet going by these guidelines alone can lead to a miserable state of sadness because most likely they will lead you to fail.

So many of us feel like we never get anywhere and we keep running in circles with no real accomplishments. You're stuck and this is often how a depressed person feels. This cycle can be detrimental to happiness. Yet, the remedy is simple. There is one key component to a good goal that most of us leave out. In order for a goal to be a good goal you have to have control over it. Yes, control. We all chase dreams and (bad) goals we have no control over. If there is no control then how can one logically justify success or failure?

So what is a good goal? In the simplest of terms let's look at some goals a sales person might have. The following would be a typical goal: I want to sell 10 widgets every day.

Sounds like a great goal, right? Absolutely not. This is a horrible goal and will only lead to frustration and a sense of failure. The goal is horrible because you have no control over whether someone buys a widget from you. You could be the most persuasive sales person in the world and you still have no control over this goal. So how would you reformulate this into a great goal? Let's try this: I will make 20 phone calls to 20 new prospects each day. Now, this is a great goal! The sales person has 100% control over whether he picks up the telephone and makes the calls!

Now, you are probably thinking, I'm not a sales person with quotas to fulfill. I'm a depressed person so how does this apply to my life and my happiness? Well, I believe it is the secret to happiness. Let's look at it from another perspective. Maybe you want to lose weight. What would a good goal be?

Lose 10 pounds in three months.

or

Change all bread and pasta products I eat to whole wheat and walk two miles each day.

The first statement is not a good goal. It is a wish or a desire because you have no control over it. However, the second statement is a great goal for losing weight because not only is it specific and has associated times but you have complete control over all aspects of it.

So now that you know the definition and structure of a real goal how do you apply it to your life and your overall happiness? How will goals lead to your happiness? Here are five ways to start letting goals lead to happiness in your life. Look at your life and examine changes you wish to make. Prioritize these desires. Take the top three and write three real goals to achieve them. We all have ups and downs in our life. We experience good times and we have to maneuver through bad times too. Some of us have a fairly easy time coming through the bad times while others of us suffer from anxiety and depression. No matter where you fall on the spectrum make goals to help you deal with bad times in the future. Here are some good goals to lead to contentment.

1) I will begin and end each day with a prayer.

and

2) When I feel sad I will write a list of what is making me sad and organize them into categories: The ones I have control over and the ones I do not have control over.

It is scientifically proven that exercise makes us feel better. It releases endorphins, assists with stress management and can add to our happiness. So, create a goal for exercise.

3) I will walk one mile each evening.

Resist the comfort that a stagnant life can form. It's so easy to stay in the safety of your comfort zone. But, one must continue to grow. You must strive to learn new things. It could be to read the book you've been thinking about reading for months. Start a garden or go to that cooking class you've always wanted to attend.

4) Set a goal to learn or try one new thing each month. *and*

5) Make it a goal to start and end each day on a positive note by reading an inspirational quote or scripture before you get out of bed in the morning and before you close your eyes at night.

Now, think about what you have just read. Examine your current goals. Are they good ones? If not, reconstruct them or change them completely. For all of your goals, get on your feet and start working towards them. For everything else get on your knees and start praying.

I came across the following poem and unfortunately, I do not know the author so I am unable to give them credit. Whoever you are, thank you! This poem is a prayer and I think it is a great "example" of the marriage of excellent, healthy goals and the power of prayer as God intended. I encourage you to meditate on these words and their purpose and then apply them to your prayers and your goals.

A Beautiful Prayer

I asked God to take away my pain.
God said, No.
It is not for me to take away,
But for you to give it up.

I asked God to make my handicapped child whole.
God said, No.
Her spirit was whole,
Her body was only temporary.

I asked God to grant me patience.
God said, No.
Patience is a byproduct of tribulations;
It isn't granted, it is learned.

I asked God to give me happiness.
God said, No.
I give you blessings.
Happiness is up to you.

I asked God to spare me pain.
God said, No.
Suffering draws you apart from worldly cares and

Brings you closer to me.

I asked God to make my spirit grow.
God said, No.
You must grow on your own,
But I will prune you to make you fruitful.

I asked for all things that I might enjoy life.
God said, No.
I will give you life so that
You may enjoy all things.

I ask God to help me LOVE others,
As much as he loves me.
God said…Ahhhh,
Finally you have the idea.

8) Growing Into Depression

I've been escaping since I was a child. When I was little I couldn't pronounce any "r" or "s" sounds. It was so bad that no one could understand me except for my mom. I shied away from speaking to anyone because it became so frustrating. I started going to Speech Class (or peach as I called it) before I even entered kindergarten. I guess this was one of my first escapes. I loved "peach". My teacher was Miss "A" and our classes were one on one. That's still where I operate at my best, either one on one or in a small group.

Slowly but surely Miss "A" taught me how to

speak coherently and wow did that drown out my shyness! I became an avid little sales lady while in elementary school. I sold greeting cards to every woman at church, earning me money and prizes along the way. My brother ignited my competitive spirit and I was determined to do anything and everything he did and to do it better. This naturally transformed into a love of sports where luckily for the most part I flourished. Through the years depression has diluted my passion for competition.

Growing up if I wasn't on a basketball court or a softball field, you could find me in our tree house or in my closet. Usually, I'd have a book in my hands. Playing ball I was the most competitive, go getter, outspoken gal you could find. Once, my foot stepped off the court I would be the exact opposite. I transformed my closet into a hideaway. I took everything out from the top shelf, going across the length of the closet. I used the center shelves that my dad had constructed as a ladder to climb up to my homemade fort. I spent hours up there reading and writing. Imagining. My other escape was our tree house. No matter where we lived dad always built us an outdoor fort. We'd play in there no matter if it were cold or hot. It was my direct route into other worlds.

It's as if when I was a child I lived in a world of opposites. I was either an extremely competitive person or a reclusive shy girl. Don't think I was this odd child that stood out in crowds. I was very normal, exceeding in most I did and even being social with girlfriends, having slumber parties, and best friends. But I think the patterns of depression started planting their seeds when I was young. As I grew older I still had friends but fewer than before. I cared less about social activities and I continued down my path to solitude.

In first grade, there were six or seven girls in class that sat next to each other, including me. The classroom was actually a converted teacher's lounge, the joys of growing up in a small town! One afternoon the entire group of girls got in trouble for talking so under teacher orders we started back on our papers. What do first graders talk about anyway? Typical of girls, some of them started talking again. The teacher was furious and we had ignited her short fuse. The result was our recess was taken away. I was so irritated that I promptly walked up to her and told her I wasn't talking so it wasn't fair. Can you see a first grade little girl known for being shy being so determined! She wouldn't listen and refused to change her mind. Fuming, I went back to my seat. I couldn't sit still and I was getting angrier by the second. Stubbornness happens to be another family trait!

About five minutes passed and then my little arm rose up. When the teacher saw my hand extended she acknowledged me and I asked to go to the restroom. She said yes and I lifted from my seat, left the classroom and took a left down the hallway towards the bathroom. But, instead of taking the last corner to the girls' room I kept on my straight path and walked directly past the principal's office, out the school's front double doors, down the sidewalk, across the road to our house, through our fence into our backyard and climbed into our fort with my dog Smokey! I never hesitated and I was determined to prove my teacher wrong! Does that sound like a girl on the road to depression? The only connection I can find is that even as a little girl I wasn't concerned about the other girls but I was overwhelmingly worried about doing something bad and not measuring up to high standards.

Our fort was an old swing set that my dad had transformed by adding wood panels and forming a teepee looking structure with a pointed roof and two sloping sides. The ends were blocked off and there was a small opening at one end big enough for us to squeeze through. It also served as our Collie-German Shepherd mix, Smokey's home. My love of dogs has grown by leaps and bounds over the years!

So I plopped my little butt down on the floor and curled up with Smokey. I do not know how much time passed before they found me but it seemed like at least a couple hours. Can you imagine if that happened today? The troops would probably be called in! My stubborn attitude paid off. After I was found, I didn't get in trouble by mom and dad or by the school. I did have to miss my recess but they gave a special project to tackle. I was happy! So, you can see that stubbornness and a strong will were in my blood from the very beginning. You can also see that I had very wise parents who knew the value of the lesson I learned was greater than any punishment might have taught me.

I recently saw a story on the Today Show about a girl who couldn't get rid of the hiccups. That was me in second grade. Mysteriously I would get the hiccups every day following lunch. They were so big, loud and obnoxious and they happened every single day after lunch. It became so disruptive to the class that I was sent into the hallway until the hiccups would pass. It was so automatic that I didn't even wait for the hiccups to present themselves. I just grabbed my desk after lunch and marched to the hall.

Being in the hall wasn't a horrible occurrence because I was left alone to do my work and read. I liked doing both of those things even at that young age. And, I could find peace within the hallway. The hiccups would last at least thirty minutes and sometimes longer than an hour. That wasn't even bad. The bad thing, the really bad thing was while I was sitting in the hall, day after day, the third graders would walk by returning from their lunch. That was the bad part. They would laugh at me every day. I would try so hard not to hiccup as they walked by but it never worked. So, I avoided eye contact at all costs. I can see their little squirmy faces giggling and their fingers stretching out pointing at my face. It certainly didn't help my social skills but it made me more resilient and stubborn. I got to the point where ninety nine percent of me didn't care about the pointing fingers or cackles. But, no one can completely resign themselves from caring.

As I grew older I became bored at school. I had always been bored. At one point I was instructed to go to the counselor's office and was forced to take all of these weird tests. I wasn't for sure why I was taking the tests but I enjoyed the break from the monotonous classroom activities and it was a new challenge. The tests went on for several days. I thought it might have something to do with my boredom but wasn't for sure. I was simply happy for the change of pace. I started snooping in on adult conversations and finally concluded that the school was considering creating a special class for me and the other bored kids. I wasn't for sure what this meant but I kept having to retake all of the tests. At first, I didn't understand but soon I realized I had to take them over and over because I wasn't doing well enough. My grade on the test wasn't cutting it.

I was never told that I wasn't good enough but that's my first memory of failure. I knew my parents wanted me to do better but I also knew they weren't disappointed in me. They fought for me. I ended up in that "gifted" class, not because of my high scores or lack thereof, but because my parents fought for what they knew was best for me. They paved my way. I know they prayed continually about me and my brother and they continue to do so.

Anything I've managed to succeed at in life can be contributed to my mom and dad. They've provided the perfect combination of love, guidance and discipline. Beyond that they have been the consistent compass and example of parents and partners living their life together for God. God blessed me deeply by letting me be born into a safe, strong and Godly family.

Both mom and dad have had to deal with a parent who committed suicide and live with the knowledge that many of their loved ones struggle with depression. My mom is plagued with debilitating migraines, cluster headaches and fibromyalgia. I'm convinced that these are caused by or linked to depression. But she is a fighter! Her strength and determination amaze me.

My dad is the strongest yet gentlest; the wisest yet most humble man I know. He has his moments too. The moments shake my heart every time. He is in his 60s and is still an avid softball player. His team of sixty year olds travels on a regular basis to states across the country to compete. I hope I can be doing such a thing at that age. I'm very proud of him. However, sometimes the certainty of his age beginning to limit his abilities can really take its toll. It scares me to think how he might react to this reality in years to come. His father ultimately committed suicide based on the abilities that cancer had taken away from him.

I cannot give my parents enough compliments to describe how wonderful they truly are. I can't explain the hurt it causes me and my brother to see them hurt, whether caused by the repercussions of depression or something else. In some ways they have it worse than anyone. They have had to come to grips with their parents' suicides and also see both of their children deal with depression.

Even though school was boring I loved the act of learning. I still do. My love for reading began in kindergarten. The front corner of my kindergarten school room had been transformed into a little nook with a carpeted floor and bookshelves inviting you into a multitude of worlds. It was such a comforting feeling. That's where I escaped to as a little girl. It was much easier to have fun with books and engage in learning than to initiate friendships with other boys and girls.

At the age of five, I was more concerned with getting 100% on papers, compliments from the teacher and finishing faster than my peers than I was concerned about other kids or making friends. And, my best friend in kindergarten ended up moving to another school making it even worse. When I was with friends we would spend a lot of time outside exploring and playing on the swing set. It was also cool to live right across the street from the school because we were only steps away from a full allotment of entertainment. It was a major score for a little kid.

I discovered one of the most valuable life lessons as a fourth grader: pray for your enemies! Before your head hits your pillow tonight pray for the Lord to give you the strength to face your friends and your enemies this week with God's character as your shield. And, even more important, pray that your enemies are happy! Pray that He gives you peace in your struggles, insight in your confusion and direction in your ways. Girls can be brutal, especially pre-teen hormonal girls!

Fourth grade was the year I discovered basketball. I began to see how I was wired differently than the other girls. All I cared about was winning. I could care less about the social aspect or the pizza parties. All I wanted to do was be the best basketball player ever and win every game. In between games and before and after practice the other girls would be goofing off. I was always just a little uncomfortable during these times. You could find me on the court shooting free throws.

Part of this behavior was because I just wasn't comfortable in that environment. I've never understood it. Like a turtle I'd crawl in under my shell becoming very hesitant to chime in and contribute to the fun. But now, I wonder if part of it was genetics. If I was already showing signs of my own depression? I was isolating myself and I was ultra-competitive. Both of these are traits of my family and our shared depression.

It was really ironic because the popular girls saw me as a threat. This was something I didn't comprehend. All I wanted was to play ball and be alone. In fact, I was actually scared to death of it! I've never been able to comprehend why people worry so much about what other people think of them. Who cares! But, it did create a hellish environment at times especially for a pre-teen girl.

All of these occurrences and choices were like seeds planting the chance for depression to grow. As a child I began avoiding social interaction. I sought out seclusion and escaped in the form of books and ball courts. Individually, the seeds were very small and insignificant. It took a long time for them to take root and grow but they were planted in fertile ground when I was that little girl. You can find many examples of the power and strength of seeds in the Bible. God uses the mustard seed to demonstrate the power of faith and he uses the example of weeds to explain the contagious effects of sin.

9) Growing Up Depressed

Teenage years can be tough. *"Don't let anyone look down on you because you are young, but set an example for the believers in speech, in life, in love, in faith and in purity,"* 1 Timothy 4:12 NIV. As a teenager the theme continued, I never cared whether I was popular or not. Rather I was focused on excelling in the classroom and at sports. It was very important for me to make my parents proud. It is even to this day and will be until I die. I was very focused on my goals including my grades and my college ambitions.

You see, none of these things are weird. They are probably pretty normal for a lot of people but for me, all of these lifestyle choices not only had to do with my personality but they were rooted in my genetic code. If one examines these personality traits and choices one will discover that they all paved a way for me to escape. There's nothing wrong with these but for me they were the first inlets to depression. Curious how you can be so ambitious but have depression? One would think the two couldn't coexist.

I might have been bored during my elementary days but I hated high school. It was full of catty girls lurching in the hallways, popularity contests and stupid stuff I cared less about. I didn't even like girls when I was young, let alone when many turned to "witches". Sometimes I would dread the passage down the hall filled with whispers, rolling eyes and smirks. I was very involved in sports and clubs, yet, I wasn't popular in the least of ways. I wouldn't call myself unpopular either, if that makes any sense. I've always gotten along with boys better than girls. It's easier to have a conversation and let my guard down because you can talk about sports and other subjects where there are no true feelings attached. I really have to work to develop an authentic relationship with another woman and truly become her friend. It is one thing that I deeply wish came easier to me because I know the rewards would be great.

I was extremely quiet and boys liked me because I excelled at sports, I was a tomboy and I wasn't horrible to look at for a teenage girl. That all sounds great but it was a bad combination because when you add those factors to the quiet part, girls just assume you are stuck up and I felt like I stood out like a sore thumb. I became a target of the popular girls. I survived because I developed skills to ignore them and I never allowed them to raise a reaction out of me so they bored and moved onto other distractions. I just really didn't care so there was no reason for reaction. Somehow, I was elected to the homecoming court my senior year, which I still don't understand. What didn't surprise me was getting accused of trying to stuff the ballots! You've got to be kidding me. The irony is so funny because I DIDN'T CARE AT ALL!

Instead of wasting my time caring about the highly important social circles that can only be found in high school I focused all my energy on sports and grades. I wasn't anti-social but it was pretty normal to find my head in a book instead of gossiping with the girls on the bus, on the way to the game. What did I care about in high school?

1. I cared about excelling on the volleyball court

2. I cared about getting good grades.

3. I cared about going to college

4. I cared about my boyfriend.

5. And, I cared about making my mom and dad proud of me.

1. The Volleyball Court.

Throughout life I have spent thousands of hours in a gym. I absolutely loved it. I've always wondered how a depressed person can be so competitive. I started playing volleyball in 8th grade. I became entrenched with the game as a freshman. For as many hours spent on the court throughout high school and later in college it's sad that the time spent with teammates didn't result in even one authentic friend. Yes, I consider many of them friends and I would be genuinely excited if I ran into them by happenstance. Yet, I do not continually communicate with any of them. It occurs to me that starting at a young age I never developed the skill of "making friends". This weakness reared up greatly in the social institution called high school. I believe this lack of skill or refusal to allow others in is directly related to my depression.

Throughout four entire years of volleyball I had the same practice partners. We did every drill together and warmed up together before every game. Off court, we probably spoke less than 100 words to each other in four years. She was the queen of the social ladder and that ladder wasn't even on my radar.

My focus on the volleyball court led to numerous championships, conference, district and state recognitions and ultimately a full ride college scholarship. Volleyball was really my life. I lived for it. I couldn't understand why the other girls weren't as intense as me. I didn't care about anything else. My senior year was all about making it to State. I was so focused and goal oriented at that time. Over the years this part of my personality has diminished. Depression has taken hold of part of my determination. We made it to State that year. Goal accomplished.

The court was a great exodus for me. The focus was on competition. Goals of improving and winning trumped all other motivations. Little social interaction was necessary. In retrospect, sports provided the same shelter for me as the diversion of books. Sports masked my insecurities allowing me to excel without spotlighting my weaknesses.

2. Good Grades.

I was determined to get A's. Achieving a lovely "B" was not an option. Starting in kindergarten I was unwavering in my pursuit. As each year past the classes gradually got harder and I had to work harder and longer. While many things came easy to me on the learning curve I wouldn't describe myself as a natural. I worked tirelessly to get the grade.

The key to my academic achievements was memorization. I learned early on that if I wrote it down I would remember it. My writing hand got very sore throughout high school and even more so during college. And, I do not even hold my pencil correctly!

There is one high school math class I particularly remember because I know I did not earn an "A" even though that beautiful letter ended up on my report card. The teacher was notorious for opening all the windows when the thermometer read 15 degrees and snow was falling on the ground. Students would arrive to class bundled head to toe with winter coats, gloves and scarves.

I would pray every day that he wouldn't call me to the board. It was dreadful. Sometimes you would stand there the entire hour exasperated and feeling dumb not knowing how to solve the equation and the teacher not offering to help. I guess he was trying to teach via humiliation! I remember one girl bursting into tears, running from the room and not stopping until she was safely seated in the counselor's office.

I utterly dreaded the delivery of my grade card. It caused my level of stress to elevate off the scale. My pursuit to avoid failure overpowered all other concerns. The only way I saw the "A" on my report card had to be his measurement of my effort and desire.

I had no idea the seeds of depression were slowly growing inside of me during my days of youth. I had no knowledge of the genetics I acquired or my family's history. My first confrontation with depression was my Grandpa's suicide.

Looking back at the days of my youth I wonder if my shyness and social seclusion had anything to do with depression or if it was merely part of my introverted personality. No matter the reason, no matter what I was going through I know God was with me, using these experiences to mold me into what He wanted me to become. *"He gives strength to the weary and increases the power of the weak. Even youths grow tired and weary, and young men stumble and fall; but those who hope in the LORD will renew their strength. They will soar on wings like eagles; they will run and not grow weary, they will walk and not be faint,"* Isaiah 40:29-31 NIV.

3. College Bound.

Depressed or not, one thing I've always been is goal-driven. High school was only an obstacle I had to hurdle over to arrive at college. Goals have always been excessively important to me. As I've gained a tiny ounce of wisdom throughout the years I realized even more so how important goals are for the depressed. Goals create energy, focus and determination. I've developed a new outlook on spiritual goals. Most importantly, you must have them!

My goals were typical for a high school kid. Go to college. Win the game. Make my boyfriend love me. Avoid my brother! These are typical, yet nothing but horrible goals. The main reason they are bad is because you have no control over the goals and you have no control over others.

I was an overachiever in high school aspiring to be an over-achieving college student. I achieved that goal. In college I had two majors and a minor, I was the captain of the volleyball team, editor of the yearbook, Communication Student of the year, worked in the Public Relations Office, and had an off campus job. However, it was a very telling tale. For me, boredom breeds depression. When I'm challenged and busy, my mood tends to lift. When one closely examines the list of activities they'll notice that none of them are cemented in social activity. My busyness was actually breeding my depression.

4. *First Love*

Yes, I like all other teenage girls to come before and after, was struck by the hormone induced love bug only as a teenager can experience. Of course, I thought we were perfect for each other and we would be together forever. And of course I was wrong. However, we were together for almost four years which I would guess is above average for most teenage relationships. It was great at the time until he broke my heart and it cemented many of my habits of depression I wasn't aware of at the time. In that relationship I had created a world of comfort in one person and saw no need to seek other friendships or social interactions. I was either with him, on a gym floor or had my head in a book.

As with any teenage love, I thought it was forever. We would grow up, get married and live in happily-ever-after-land. Wow, was I wrong. I'm so glad I was wrong. Looking back there was no way in an adult relationship he could have dealt with my resoluteness!

But he broke my heart. Even though I knew it wasn't God's plan for us to be together. I couldn't let go so I allowed him to break my heart. Without him I felt awkward and out of place. Kind of like a smoker not knowing what to do with their hand when it isn't holding a cigarette. I didn't want to put out the social effort to create other relationships. The idea of being with him was easy and comforting. If I didn't move on then there was no chance for more hurt or rejection.

The one absolute result of our relationship was a broken heart. My heart. Not only did my heart ache but my comfort zone was obliterated. I had to reassess my social realm and venture into new ways to spend my time and new people to spend it with. Again, lack of focus and lack of activity opens the door for depression. The door swung wide open leading me to bad choices. They weren't detrimental choices, rather ones many college age kids make. But, the point here is for someone with the tendency for depression the door doesn't just creep open, it is kicked wide open.

After the break up was when I first experienced moments and minutes of my mind going dull (or at least the first dull moments I remember). Minutes would go by without really knowing what I had thought about, a hidden haze. If I wasn't busy being busy this fuzzy place was a retreat of comfort. To this day I often vacation in this far off place of luxury only located in my mind. I can be sitting in a room full of people entrenched in conversation yet be a world away. I'm very good at disguising my mind because nobody has a clue. I'm in a far-away-land.

5. *Making Mom and Dad Proud*

My parents have always been the supporting foundation I've needed. Look to your family and friends for help. They want to help you but you have to open the door and invite them in. No matter what struggle you face remember that Jesus knows your heart. He is there. Draw on Him for strength. Draw on those around you for support.

As an adult, I know how truly unique my family is and, that's a good thing! Even as a teenager I liked my parents. How many teens could truly say they liked spending time with mom and pop? They've always been my best friends, whom I can depend on for anything. They are absolutely a living testimony to faith, courage and Christian consistency.

Our house wasn't a quiet house but there was no yelling. Discipline and disappointment didn't come in the form of loud voices. In fact, I can only remember a handful of disagreements between any of us. You knew Dad was upset if he leaned his chin down into his neck and started a conversation with the words, "Now, Jana…..." in a deep, solid and overly concerned voice. I can hear it today! On the other hand you could always hear booming laughter and cackles created from lively conversations, joking around and friendly competition.

In some ways our home was very strict but there weren't many rules. We were taught right from wrong and what was expected of us and we simply did it. If we didn't, we knew more than being in trouble we would be disappointing mom and dad. That was the most horrible feeling in the world. It is today, even as an adult, a guiding light within my life.

Our house was a very happy house. We weren't rich but we were abundantly blessed with healthy, loving and supportive parents. My mom and dad never missed a single volleyball or basketball game I ever played in. That includes every game I ever played while in elementary, junior high, high school and even college. Simply amazing!

Looking back I was probably a weirdo in high school! Popularity wasn't a priority to me. I was quiet. Often my quiet nature was misinterpreted as a "higher" than thou attitude. I probably fed this misconception because I never felt it worth the energy to refute. I was rarely invited to "cool" parties but I didn't care. I wasn't into drinking or drugs or anything like that. I just went along my merry way waiting for the whole experience to be over.

I was a loner but I was never alone! I always knew there was something bigger and better waiting around the corner. I have no doubt that God had a plan for me and still does today but I often have a hard time deciphering the details of that plan. Do you ever struggle with this? I pray that I'm taking the steps He wants me to take but sometimes self-doubt takes over. Am I really listening to Him or are my human ways interfering with what He wants? Even when I feel the closest to God I still wonder if I'm traveling down the path He desires for me.

I believe the best way to insure I'm doing what He wants me to do is to pray about it and read about it. *"No eye has seen, no ear has heard, no mind has conceived what God has prepared for those who love him but God has revealed it to us by his Spirit. The Spirit searches all things, even the deep things of God,"* 1 Corinthians 2:9-10 NIV.

May your future no longer be full of "what if's."

May it from now on be full of forward motion guided and inspired by God. Recently during a sermon the preacher, Jerry introduced me to the inspiring words of Matthew West's song, *"Motion"*. The song's words show that God has a plan for you and it is a deliberate plan. He doesn't want you to simply go through the motions. He has given you a purpose.

This might hurt, it's not safe
But I know that I've gotta make a change
I don't care if I break,
At least I'll be feeling something
'Cause just okay is not enough
Help me fight through the nothingness of life

I don't wanna go through the motions
I don't wanna go one more day
without Your all consuming passion inside of me
I don't wanna spend my whole life asking,
"What if I had given everything,
instead of going through the motions?"

No regrets, not this time
I'm gonna let my heart defeat my mind

Let Your love make me whole
I think I'm finally feeling something
'Cause just okay is not enough
Help me fight through the nothingness of this life

'Cause I don't wanna go through the motions
I don't wanna go one more day
without Your all consuming passion inside of me
I don't wanna spend my whole life asking,
"What if I had given everything,
instead of going through the motions?"

take me all the way (take me all the way)
take me all the way ('cause I don't wanna go through the motions)
take me all the way (I know I'm finally feeling something real)
take me all the way

I don't wanna go through the motions
I don't wanna go one more day
without Your all consuming passion inside of me
I don't wanna spend my whole life asking,
"What if I had given everything,
instead of going through the motions?"

I don't wanna go through the motions
I don't wanna go one more day
without Your all consuming passion inside of me

Remember that we are not alone in our walk. Jesus even gave up his glory to tread the same roads we walk along. It has always been very hard for me to grasp the fact (and yes it is a fact) that Jesus was really human and He knows what we are going through. But He did experience all the trials, temptations, sadness and grief that we experience. It might be the shortest verse in the Bible but it is very significant – *"Jesus wept,"* John 11:35. The night before the crucifixion He pleaded to the Lord to find another way. He fell on his face to pray to the Lord asking to, "Let this cup pass from Me." He begged of the apostles to stay with Him, saying, "My soul is deeply grieved, to the point of death; remain here and keep watch with Me," Matthew 26:38-44 NASB.

10) Being A Depressed Adult

These patterns of focusing my energy on goals, drawing inward, avoiding relationships and slowly falling down the tunnel of depression continued as I entered college. My competitive drive earned me both volleyball and academic scholarships. I chose to live at home the first year because I couldn't imagine living in a claustrophobic dormitory filled with lively conversations, drama and all-hour unending energy.

I made friends with some of the volleyball girls. Unfortunately, during my freshman year, most of the upper classmen were more focused on drinking, smoking and partying than they were on volleyball so that didn't encourage too much bonding for me. I was usually very quiet on the road trips, diving my nose into a text book and sometimes even avoiding eye contact. I haven't managed to keep in touch with any of the girls who were my friends (except through Facebook which doesn't require any social interaction; just a computer). I guess that's kind of normal, yet I feel like it is my fault. My lack of effort to actually cement long term relationships is 100% my fault. I don't like letting people in. Outside of my family very few people really know me.

I've never been good at making friends. I'm very good at being friendly but to actually trust and share with people, not so much. I'm very, very selective. I don't even like going to friends' houses for get-togethers. I fret about going to bunko parties, Avon sales and baby showers. Sometimes I have a wonderful time but generally I just want to go home as soon as I get there. Sometimes I don't care that I feel this way but mostly it makes me feel weird and horrible. It's hard to understand why I wouldn't want to have fun like everyone else. It's hard for me to both give and receive love. Vulnerability is a place I try to avoid.

Do you have love in your life? Do you give love to others? Do you have a husband or wife who is your best friend? Do you have friends who have your best interest at heart? Do you accept God's love? If you said no to any one of these questions then I would say you have depression seeping into your heart, soul and mind. Love is the most powerful emotion God has given us. When you give or receive love your body explodes with endorphins! If there is love in your life there must be some happiness in your life. If you aren't letting love into your life examine the reasons why and take steps to fix it.

In college I was on my first losing volleyball team ever, my boyfriend broke up with me and broke my heart, I got my first "C" and I met my first husband who eventually cheated on me multiple times. That would make anyone depressed!

It wasn't all bad! But, I would say it was atypical of the college perception of parties, good times and fun.

My social awkwardness made its official debut during college. I wasn't close to my high school friends. The majority of the volleyball team whom I spent ninety percent of my time with had different priorities and values than me. Plus, there was a huge division between upper and lower classmen on the team. There were two other freshmen on the volleyball team so we clung together but I never got close to them. We supported each other through the season and the year. We looked out for one another and we protected each other.

But that's as far as the relationship ever went. Intimacy never flourished between us as a genuine friendship provides. However in that setting and at that time they did provide support. That is as far as I would let them in. I missed out on many great experiences and friendships because I never took my wall down.

No matter if you are in a time of trial or a time of joy I cannot express how important it is to have a support system. I can testify about this because I admit how bad I am at doing it! I recently ran my first 5K. I would have never done this if it wasn't for my sister-n-law. (Thank you, Holly!) Three of us took the journey together as we trekked the three plus miles. We had a fabulous time and not only was it beneficial to our bodies but it was beneficial to our souls. *"Whoever walks with the wise becomes wise, but the companion of fools will suffer harm,"* Proverbs 13:20 ESV.

The friends I have today I treasure dearly. As I get older, I realize how important friendships are to our spiritual well-being. Quantity of friendships is not important but having authentic friendships is very important. God made it very clear that we need to be around people who have the same beliefs as we do or we are likely to fall.

When we do fall, a friend is who we need to pick us up and carry us through. Who are your friends? Are they supportive or are they toxic? Pray to God about your friends. Pray for the growth of your friendships, for healthy, strong and encouraging friends. Give praise to God for the authentic friends you have! *"Where there is no guidance, a person falls, but in an abundance of counselors there is safety,"* Proverbs 11:14 KJV.

The lack of intimacy within my friendships and the general college environment opened the door for me to draw within myself for the first time as an adult. I realized that I was and still am very comfortable just being by myself. While this obviously doesn't make one depressed, if you are prone to depression it can provide the opportunity it needs to move into your life. It's as if all the moments in my life have been stepping stones covered with depression but they were strategically placed by God to slowly get me where I am today. God can work through your depression and create amazing things if you let Him. Not only will he get you through it He'll make sure good comes out of it.

I met my first husband in college. I hate even saying that but it is what it is. It still drastically bothers me that I'm divorced. We married the summer after I graduated college and I moved to Kansas City to start our new life together. Our marriage ended abruptly after about three years when I discovered through the very dependable US Mail system that he was taking a loan out to buy a car for his girlfriend.

In the next several days that went on minute by grueling minute I discovered he had actually cheated on me with numerous women. Shell shocked doesn't begin to describe my state of mind. Luckily our divorce proceeded rather quickly and God answered my prayers in getting my house sold and moving back to my hometown.

It took me over a year to recover. I still can't comprehend how someone who swears they love you and promised to protect you can do something so utterly disgusting and hurtful. The only logical explanation is he never loved me. That's a harsh reality too. I felt like I had wasted years of my life away. Recovering from this ultimate betrayal was devastatingly hard. It shook me. It was the first time I took antidepressants. It wasn't a good experience! They made me crave sleep. I quickly aborted the pills and with the support of my family slowly moved forward with my life.

If one word could describe my feelings during this time it would be fear. Fear of what happened. Fear of the future. Fear of the unknown. Did God use this experience for His good? I believe so. It made me stronger. It made me rely on Him more. And, while I was in Kansas City I met one of my best friends, an authentic friend. She's someone I can be completely raw and open with and I pray that I've made a positive impact on her life. God used a situation I could see nothing but negative in and He produced positive outcomes.

To this day if I were to cross paths with my ex I would slug him in the gut . . . maybe. When I was going to a counselor soon after discovering my husband was cheating on me the counselor kept urging me to get angry. I couldn't even say the word angry. I always used the word "mad". I really never got angry. If I would have been more assertive maybe I wouldn't still have nightmares of my ex hurting me. If I was totally honest I would admit that I wouldn't throw a single punch. Depression can rob you of true emotion.

What is the moral of the story? God gives us each the chance to start over! You can be anywhere in your life, the lowest of the lowest points and God will let you start over. God also takes what we believe to be weaknesses and he transforms them into strengths and ways to praise Him and bring others to Him.

You have a chance to start over right now! You have a chance to take something in your life that you don't like or something you think is a weakness and you can pray that God uses it to bring glory to Him! I challenge you to pray to God about using you, yes you, to change the lives of others!

I have found, me included, that many suffering from depression would rather suffer in silence than to deal with confrontation. Why do we not stand up for ourselves? Why do we have such little self-respect? Our encounters with negativity usually get swept under the rug. We keep sweeping until there's no room left under the rug and we explode. This process has to be replaced with self-respect! Respect yourself enough to stand up for yourself! It's okay! Healthier and happier relationships will be your result. You are God's creation. Treat yourself accordingly.

One trait of my personality was firmly cemented

into my being during college. I'm at my best when busy. If I'm not busy overloaded with goals and to do lists I quickly become bored and lackadaisical, cracking the window open to the wind of depression. I finished my senior year of college traveling with the volleyball team, an on campus job, an off campus job, eighteen hours of classes, applying for "real" jobs, finishing the college yearbook and planning a wedding. Phew! You can get tired just thinking about it.

Crazy, huh? It got me wondering if being busy is really good. Are you happy when you are busy? When I'm busy I feel a sense of accomplishment. When I slow down I tend to get a bit apathetic and depression seeps in. God has given us only 24 hours in each day and a definitive yet unknown amount of days. Wasting them would be a sin but being busy for the sake of being busy can be just as bad.

The following is one of my favorite stories from the Bible because it reminds me of what is really important to Jesus and being busy isn't at the top of His list!

"As Jesus and his disciples were on their way, he came to a village where a woman named Martha opened her home to him. She had a sister called Mary, who sat at the Lord's feet listening to what he said. But Martha was distracted by all the preparations that had to be made. She came to him and asked, "Lord, don't you care that my sister has left me to do the work by myself? Tell her to help me!"

"Martha, Martha," the Lord answered, "you are worried and upset about many things, [42] but few things are needed—or indeed only one. Mary has chosen what is better, and it will not be taken away from her," Luke 10:38-42 NIV.

Martha must have thought very highly of herself because she was busy cleaning the house, preparing the food and sweeping off the front porch readying her house for Jesus. From the outside looking in, especially from our Western bastardized view of time management, Mary looked very lazy and maybe even selfish. She wasn't helping with the chores and when Jesus arrived she made sure she was front and center.

Can't you imagine Martha getting miffed and whispering in the corner to others about her lazy sister? Steam was probably starting to squirt out of her ears! However, Jesus had the exact opposite reaction. Mary came straight to Him and made sure He was welcomed properly and she was intently listening to His words. Her focus was on Him and Him alone.

How are you spending your time? Are you too busy with daily chores and schedules to take time for what is really important? I've always believed it is very easy to determine a person's priorities. You simply have to see how they spend their time. How will you spend your time this week? Remember there are only 24 precious hours each day so cherish them and respect them.

"Show me, LORD, my life's end
and the number of my days;
let me know how fleeting my life is.
You have made my days a mere handbreadth;
the span of my years is as nothing before you.
Everyone is but a breath," Psalm 39:4-5 NIV.

College really brought out my love for writing. Not so much as a creative outlet because I've never been one with the ability or talent to invent stories but I found that I liked writing fiction. I went to a liberal arts school and assignments included a plethora of research papers. I not only didn't mind writing them, I actually enjoyed the process.

I've always liked to read and learn so the research part came naturally. I would attack the writing portion as it if were a puzzle. I would write sections and then move them around until the order made sense to me. Putting the puzzle pieces together was challenging and fulfilling.

I know now that God was preparing me to start my blog and write this book. Writing this book and my blog have been tremendously joyful. Being able to communicate something so personal has made me jump out of my comfort zone, has given me strength to go forward and hopefully can give a few other people as much joy and hope as it has given me.

During the process God has brought to life

many of my shortcomings. He has shown me the many holes in my life I was trying to fill with Earthly things. Putting it "out there" to the world has brought a realm of accountability. I firmly decided to do God's work, to open my vulnerability so He can use me for His good. I mentally make this decision each morning when I awake.

Words flow from my mind to paper but I continue to struggle everyday with creating intimacy within my relationships. I have to make it a priority and I have to allow myself to be vulnerable. It is a tangible process for me. If it wasn't then I would have no chance at success.

11) A Brother's Love

As a little girl, I adored my big brother as much as one possibly could. My nickname for him was Bubba; probably because of my struggles with the good letter "r". I would do everything he told me to do, clinging to his every word. And in big brother style, he of course would take advantage of my loyalty by telling me to do things I shouldn't. My mother would always instruct me that if I did what he told me I would get in trouble. But, I'd follow his words as if they were straight from the Bible. I was in trouble a lot and I'm sure he was in the background snickering and giggling!

We've always been close both as kids and as adults. We certainly fought a lot in traditional teenage sibling fashion. Bubba is almost four years older than me and my only sibling. It was during the teenage years that Bubba first started showing signs of the family curse. I thought he was just being a jerk! He would have a very short temper and even though I can't remember the specific words that slipped through his angry mouth I can vividly remember how hurtful they were. They could be downright cruel. I remember the tears they caused. It would be as if he didn't even know what came out of his mouth. He would always apologize after an episode and profusely explain that he didn't mean anything in a hurtful way.

Within our home he had the reputation of being a bit on the cranky side. My first recollection of this is him yelling, "Make her stop pounding on that thing," every time I practiced the piano. That actually didn't bother me because playing the piano wasn't leading the way on my top ten fun things to do!

As we both became teenagers we loved each other to death but we argued as siblings tend to do. I was at least a freshman in high school when we had a fight and he held me over the banister by my ankles! He wasn't always the easiest person to live with (I'm sure his wife can attest to that today). If I were to associate him with one of the "seven dwarfs" he would be Grumpy, but with a huge heart of gold.

This is the pattern with our guys. Overall personalities are somewhat quiet but can be outgoing, funny and very competitive. They choose activities such as hunting and different jobs that lead to many hours by themselves. And, they all express their depression with angry words. For Bubba, most of his words were directed at me and Mom. Never, to people outside the family.

Besides being a bit mischievous he was a good student and his employers raved about his hard work. It was as if he could have a split personality. Teachers, coaches and bosses consistently bragged about his work ethic, his friendly attitude and how he would go out of his way to help someone. Now, this is important: these all accurately describe my brother, however, he also had the ability to say very hurtful words, cutting through the heart and those words were usually aimed straight at the people he loved the most.

Today, I know that these hurtful words came from the depths of depression rooted in our family genes. Bubba would often say, "Well you know I didn't really mean that." Mean words often slip from the mouths of the family men. That is until they've come to terms with their own depression and agree to get help. And, they slip from my lips too.

Bubba and I are both very competitive creatures whom aim for perfection. We live in a world where the standard is perfection. If that is your goal then you will never be happy. We are bombarded by messages that our body should be perfect, we should have the perfect job, our kids should be perfect, our attitude should be perfect, etc....... It's impossible. Nobody is perfect. We all have strengths and we all have weaknesses. It is God's grace and the fact that we are made in the image of God that provide us the ability to make it through each day. I think the pursuit of perfection and the failure to reach it has played a part in my brother's depression, mine and other family members. Disappointments dwell in our brains overshadowing achievements. A dull mindset of defeat creeps in.

Bubba has always been my friend. He's always stood up for me and protected me. He got sent to the principal's office in elementary school for telling a boy to leave me alone. I think I was only in the second grade! As a teenager and an adult he has continued protecting me. I know that he's kept certain guys away from me when he thought they would hurt me. He's done many of these acts of kindness without my initial knowledge. He's a good guy. He's a wonderful guy.

One of my favorite Bubba stories is when he talked my Dad into letting me go on my first date. I think I was only fourteen at the time, eighth grade. However, I was in a sophomore math class. During that time I was pretty shy unless around someone I really knew. But, by chance a sophomore in that math class asked me out. A very popular sophomore who happened to be quite cute. At first my Dad refused, saying absolutely no way. No dating until age sixteen was the rule. But my brother and my Mom went to bat for me. It so happened that the boy was a pretty decent guy and had a great family so Bubba argued that Dad could let me go out with a good guy even though I wasn't sixteen or wait until I turned the magical age and watch me go out with a handful of losers!

It worked! I got to go on that first date. The date ended up being very uneventful. It didn't turn into a high school romance or even a second date. Like I said, I was too shy to let anyone get too close to me, especially an older boy. But, bottom line is that Bubba got me my first date.

You see Bubba's got a big heart but as he grew up it sometimes would hide in the shadows of his depression. He followed the steps of his older male relatives. He chose a career that gave him hours at a time in solitude. Just like me this solitude is a haven to him. Bubba married a wonderful girl and now has two great boys. Through the years and through his marriage Bubba has been challenged with dealing with his depression. For a long time he refused to acknowledge it existed.

Another trait that travels through my family is stubbornness and Bubba and I both inherited that one. But Bubba seemed to have received the full gamut of the family curse. Not only is he stubborn, he's reclusive, he's short tempered and can be angry. If you aren't a part of his inner world you would think he's your average go-lucky Joe. But, if you are on the inside you know something different.

At one time not so long ago I knew that his depression was affecting his wife and kids. So I reached out to him. You see, one might think duh that's what anyone would do but Bubba would never talk about the depression and would never admit he had it. We've never talked about Grandpa. I have no idea what Bubba thinks about what he did. Sometimes I think he doesn't even realize it happened let alone the ramifications of Grandpa's suicide on everyone. I guess if you can't see it in someone else it would be next to impossible to see it in yourself.

I prayed long and hard for Bubba during this time because I was convinced that he was traveling down Grandpa's road and at an accelerated pace. I was determined to not let that happen. Realizing that you have no power over the decisions or actions of others is the release of a huge burden. Giving it to God and knowing He is listening and intervening is a jubilation of emotions. But, oh is it hard!

I really didn't know what to do. I was perplexed and frustrated. I was desperate beyond words. His well-being consumed my every thought. So I did the only thing I knew I could do. I admitted that I had limited abilities to change the situation so I asked for help. I begged for help. I reached out to trusted confidants for advice and intervention. I prayed and begged God for his eternal intervention.

Even Jesus begged for God's help! How did the Lord react to Jesus' calls of desperation and pleading? The Lord had a plan for Jesus and He did not waiver from His plan, but He did give Jesus the strength to proceed by sending an angel for comfort and strength.

Isn't that what the Lord asks of you and me? We might not see the reasons we are headed down certain paths but all God asks of us is to have faith and know that He will give us the tools needed to succeed in His plan for us. God has promised to never put an obstacle in front of us that is too big for us to overcome, *"No temptation has overtaken you except what is common to mankind. And God is faithful; He will not let you be tempted beyond what you can bear. But when you are tempted He will also provide a way out so that you can endure it,"* 1 Corinthians 10:13 NIV.

I was perplexed in how I could help my brother and his family. I knew from my own depression how hard it can be to come to grips with and put your mind around. It's easy to let depression control you instead of you taking control of the depression. I did the only thing I knew to do. I prayed. Do you ever struggle in your prayers? What should I pray for? How should I pray? How long should I pray?

It is simple. Say and pray what is on your heart.

Still find it hard? Have you ever tried writing down your prayers instead of saying them? God doesn't care which way you do it! Sometimes I find it much easier and natural to write down my prayers. I like to think that I'm sitting right in front of God and we are simply having a conversation. Isn't that what is really happening? Isn't it amazing that we can do that? Don't be afraid or shy. There isn't a right or wrong way. Simply talk to Him. Talk to Him as if He's your best friend. Talk to Him as if He is your Earthly father. He is your friend and He is your father.

Don't think that prayer has to be in some formal setting or ritual such as kneeling down bedside each night. That's not a bad thing but you can pray constantly all day long. I find some of my most meaningful communication with God is throughout the day in a never ending conversation. What does the Bible say about how to pray?

Be brutally honest. It's silly that we aren't honest with God about our anger and hurt. He knows everything about us! Doesn't it make sense that we should flood these emotions to our Father instead of our brothers and sisters? Even Jesus said, *"My God, my God, why have you forsaken me?"* Matthew 27:46 NIV. He knows our fears, our temptations and our weaknesses. Jesus was here on Earth just as we are now! The Lord will never respond in rebuke to your prayers. Remember how he whispered to David and Elijah's cries for help! *"Let us then with confidence draw near to the throne of grace, that we may receive mercy and find grace to help in time of need,"* Hebrews 4:16 ESV.

Give thanks. *"I always thank my God for you and for the gracious gifts he has given you, now that you belong to Christ Jesus,"* 1 Corinthians 1:4 NIV. Be mindful of the blessings he constantly gives you. As the song says, "Count Them One by One."

Do not doubt that your prayer will be answered. *"But let him ask in faith, with no doubting, for the one who doubts is like a wave of the sea that is driven and tossed by the wind,"* James 1:6 ESV.

Pray about your troubles. *"Offer to God a sacrifice of thanksgiving, and perform your vows to the Most High, and call* *upon me in the day of trouble; I will deliver you, and you shall glorify me,"* Psalm 50:14-15 ESV.

Pray about and for your successes. *"Please, LORD, please save us. Please, LORD, please give us success,"* Psalm 118:25 NLT.

Pray for peace. *"I have told you these things, so that in me you may have peace. In this world you will have trouble. But take heart! I have overcome the world"* John 16:33.

Pray for your leaders and ones who are in power. *"First of all, then, I urge that supplications, prayers, intercessions, and thanksgivings be made for all people, for kings and all who are in high positions, that we may lead a peaceful and quiet life, godly and dignified in every way,"* Timothy 2:1-2 ESV.

Pray for those who are suffering. *"Is anyone among you suffering? Let him pray. Is anyone cheerful? Let him sing praise. Is anyone among you sick? Let him call for the elders of the church, and let them pray over him, anointing him with oil in the name of the Lord,"* James 5:13-14 ESV.

Pray about your sins. *"Therefore, confess your sins to one another and pray for one another, that you may be healed. The*

prayer of a righteous person has great power as it is working,"
James 5:16 ESV.

If you still do not know where to begin I encourage
you to try a few things:

- Read a chapter in the Bible then pray about
  what you read.
- Write down five things you are thankful for
  and then pray about them.
- Write down five things you are worried
  about and then pray about them.

No matter what keep it simple. Simply, talk to God.
Start with what is on your heart! He's waiting for you!

With a lot of prayer and conversations a miracle
happened and Bubba was able to begin to address his
struggles. It was an amazing point in both of our lives.
He probably doesn't even know the effect he's had on
me. I wouldn't have admitted to my own struggles
without witnessing his. I'm forever indebted to him. I
was and am so proud of him. I know that it was very
difficult to confront the situation but he did it head on.

He even went to a doctor and as far as I know he's still on medication which is a huge step. It's allowed his naturally big heart to shine. However, we still don't talk about it. Maybe one day we'll be able to take that step.

If you find yourself depressed, if you find yourself stricken with grief, if you find yourself just plain tired I encourage you to find strength in God's promises.

> *God hath not promised skies*
> *Always blue,*
> *Flowers-strewn pathways all*
> *Our lives through;*
> *God hath not promised sun*
> *Without rain,*
> *Joy without sorrow, peace*
> *Without pain.*
> *But God hath promised strength*
> *For the day.*
> *Rest for the labor, light for the way,*
> *Grace for the trials, help*
> *From above,*

Unfailing sympathy
Undying love…

Author Unknown

My brother has been my defender, my protector and my friend. Some might describe him as a bear on the outside and a puppy within. Anyone who really knows him knows a person with a heart of gold. As a kid I would do anything he told me to do no matter the cost. I was his constant shadow no matter how much frustration I caused him. I was determined to keep up and show up.

In a recent conversation with my Mom about Grandpa she described her dad as being a provider but that was the extent of their relationship. Few to no conversations are remembered. She knows very little about her dad. I have few memories too.

On the other hand my brother has vivid and plentiful memories of grandpa. Positive, happy memories. They shared experiences together, mostly on the water, wasting the day together under the sun fishing. These are good memories. Ones he cherishes and ones of which I am truly jealous. They are precious and private memories I would never ask Bubba to divulge. I know he has them tucked away in a very special place inside his heart.

I will go to the grave wondering why Grandpa didn't deem me special enough to share these moments. Jealousy isn't usually a sin I struggle with but I am jealous of my brother's relationship with Grandpa. Even with the jealousy I can say that I'm happy Bubba has those experiences. In an ironic way I'm sure those memories have helped Bubba maneuver through his own life, and his own struggles.

12) Make A Plan Of Action

Never allow happiness to be elusive again! Never allow depression, worry, sadness or anxiety to rule your heart and your actions. I have scanned the web, read articles in magazines, and researched medical journals and I've come to the conclusion that happiness can be found in the "Four P's". The Four P's are Plan, Passion, Power and Play. It's simple and it's easy. Follow this simple plan and start smiling! Start breathing again. Start living the life God has planned for you.

1. **Plan** *Your Life*

Do you have a plan for happiness? That sounds kind of weird doesn't it? It shouldn't be. You should have a plan for anything you want to accomplish. So if you want to be happy you need to make a plan. When creating your plan for happiness there are four areas you should focus on and we'll examine each of these now.

A. Learn to love goals.

B. *Never put all your eggs in the same basket.*

C. *Happiness: It's a Choice*

D. *Own it.*

Remember there is no reward if there is no action. In order to grow you have to stretch your limitations.

A. Learn to love goals

If I had to pick one thing that will make the most difference in anyone's happiness it is the establishment of healthy goals. We are constantly bombarded with our successes and our failures and the failures can be detrimental to our state of mind and overall health. Now, I'm not one to sugarcoat things or pretend that everything is "hunky dory". No, I'm not suggesting that. I just believe there is a right way and there is a wrong way to establish goals. And, if you establish goals in the wrong way you are setting yourself up for failure and a very unhappy life.

What are the components of a healthy goal?

1. It is detailed.
2. It is simple.
3. It has a deadline.
4. And, most importantly you have control over it.

The first three components are pretty self-explanatory and are the standard for what most people consider to be the criteria for a good goal. However, even if you meet the first three qualifications, but not the fourth, it is not a healthy goal. I know this can be a hard concept to capture so we will look at the same examples set forth in the chapter dedicated to goals. Here's a simple example that most of us can relate to: "I want to lose 10 pounds by the end of the month."

1. Is this goal detailed? It has a defined goal and it

has a deadline so I would say yes.

2. Is this goal simple? Yes, it is short and sweet.

3. Does this goal have a deadline? Yes.

4. Do you have control over this goal? Not really. We all know that sometimes we starve ourselves to death and we still don't lose a single pound.

I would say that it was a desire, not a goal. So let's try this again. Here's another goal: "I want to walk two miles each day and use whole wheat instead of white starches in my diet."

1. Is this goal detailed? Yes, it states the what, the when and the how.

2. Is this goal simple? Yes, it is also short and sweet.

3. Does this goal have a deadline? Yes, it says you must do it each day.

4. Do you have control over this goal? Yes! You do have control over this goal. You have control over whether you walk two miles each day and you have control over whether you choose wheat over white!

If you design your goals in this fashion it will have a tremendously positive effect on your life. If you choose to continue creating goals designed in the original format you will constantly be chasing dreams that you have no control over and thus will most likely become very frustrated and unhappy. Focus your energy on good goals. Let God take care of the dreams and desires you have no control over. Another way of looking at it is you need to get on your feet and start working on your goals while you need to get on your knees and start praying about your desires.

B. *Never put all your eggs in the same basket.*

This saying has been around for decades. Currently, most people associate this saying with financial investments. However, the theory can be applied to your happiness as well. First, we all need balance in our lives and if we hope one thing will bring us everything we need then we are going to be disappointed. We have the choice of where we put all of our eggs. And, we have a choice of how we treat each of those eggs. Let's examine these concepts more closely by considering two theories: 1) Sleep! I need more sleep and 2) sometimes it is all about me!

Sleep! I Need Sleep!

Nothing can get you more off balanced and affect your mental and physical well-being more than a lack of sleep. One of the best routines you can adopt is getting into bed at the same time each night and getting out of it at the same time each morning. According to medical studies, ideally we should each be getting about seven hours of sleep. If you get fewer, not only will you probably be grumpy, you are more susceptible to the common cold and to major diseases such as cancer, your reaction time is slower and your cognitive thinking ability becomes negatively altered.

But you say, "I have too much to do". And, "There are not enough hours in the day." If that is your reaction then your life is out of balance! You need to make priorities. You need to learn to say no to some commitments. And, you need to say yes to sleep each and every night. You will probably find with the adequate and routine sleep you will function at a higher level and accomplish more in a smaller amount of time.

Don't get trapped in Martha's world where being busy becomes more important than living for what is truly important.

Sometimes it is all about me!

You cannot devote all of yourself to your kids, or to a single passion, or to your mate, or to your work. It also can't all be about you. According to the good ole' dictionary balance is a state of equilibrium, a mental steadiness or emotional stability. I would like my life to possess equilibrium and having mental steadiness and emotional stability because both sound like paths to happiness. So why do we so easily get out of whack? Why do we succumb to the pressures of life, our busy schedules and other people's demands?

Some of us find it very hard to say no. Find the strength to say no and your life will become so much more stable. In fact, in some respects the inability to say no is a very selfish act because in a way you are suggesting that others can't make it without you. Yes, it's a weird concept but think about it for a minute and it will make sense.

If you are busy saying yes to everything you might even miss out on some great opportunities God has presented and planned for you. We each have strengths and weaknesses and we should focus on the strengths we possess. Other people are very good in places that you may not be. Let them do those items while you focus on your strengths. The power of the little two letter word, NO is amazing.

C. *Happiness: It's a Choice*

My Mom and Dad instilled in me that I would never have control over how people treated me or what they thought of me but I always had a choice in my reaction. If someone treated me badly or unfairly I had the choice to get mad. I could choose to mope around and be sad. Or, I could choose to not let the negative energy affect me. I could choose to be happy.

That's a simple, yet exceptionally powerful concept. Happiness is a choice. You can choose to go through life with a good attitude or a horrible one. Gretchen Rubin, author of the Happiness Project explored this subject with clarity and insight (http://www.happiness-project.com/happiness_project/2010/03/happiness-is-a-choice-true-or-false-plus-the-weekly-video.html) noting that choosing to be happy can sometimes seem like a monumental task. She encourages us to break our life down into parts so it doesn't seem so overwhelming. You can pick a time of the day that is usually frustrating to you. Concentrate on that time of the day and the routines you can change to bring you happiness.

Here's another example. Do you have a boss, a coach or a teacher who is always negative? You have to interact with this person but when confronted you always walk away feeling defeated. You have a choice in this situation. You can choose ahead of time to not let the negative energy permeate into your life. If you know when you will be together then take a deep breath, say a little prayer and go into the situation with your head held high. Walk away with a feeling of accomplishment and the choice of being happy. Don't forget to pray for the person who frustrates you. Praying for their happiness might sound strange but it can have exceptional results.

D. *Own it.*

Know who you are and don't change your

personality for someone else. Many of us tend to learn this too late in life. We each need to accept who we are and not constantly be compared to others. Absolutely no one is perfect so why should your standard be perfectionism. Each and every single one of us was created in the image of God so why would we question if we are good enough? *"People are ridiculous only when they try or seem to be that which they are not,"* –Giacomo Leopardi, Italian poet, essayist and philosopher.

Take responsibility for your life and your actions. When you take responsibility for something you also take pride in it. Pride can lead to self-confidence and a feeling of accomplishment when held in check. Take responsibility for the good things you do. It's okay to do that and you can do it without being a braggart. It's harder to take responsibility when we mess up. But, remember we are all human so we all make mistakes. When we err we also learn and we grow. Own your mistakes and you'll receive a sense of relief because you know what happens? Life goes on! You become better and stronger.

2. **Passion**. *Gotta have it.*

Passion is the second key to happiness.
Sometimes we focus so much on the big picture that we
fail to notice the wonderful small details in front of us. It
is a good practice to not always look at the garden but to
look at just one simple flower. Have a passion and
celebrate the little things in life. You are surrounded by a
multitude of blessings and each should be celebrated.
Often in the world of marketing and business people
will refer to "KISS" which means "Keep it Simple
Stupid". This can be applied to your happiness. Keep
your happiness simple starting with the simple choice to
be happy.

You must always be growing. Sometimes life can
become very stagnant, routine and dry. Learning new
things, starting new hobbies and developing new
passions is a great tool for balance in your life and
overall happiness. Don't be afraid to start something
new or venture into something you aren't 100%
comfortable with. Check with your local community
college and see if there are any classes that interest you.
Join an exercise group that holds you accountable. Look

for a book club to participate in. Start a garden and dedicate yourself to its success. The options are endless and the fun is limitless. Take the leap. That's the hardest step. Make it a goal to start something new every month and simply make yourself do it. The rewards will be bountiful.

Kind of ironic how the root of the word compassion is passion, isn't it? If you want to truly be happy then start focusing on other people's needs instead of your own. The blessings will be endless because you'll realize how fortunate you are. Doesn't it feel good to help people? The simple biblical phrase, *"Do unto others as you would have them do unto you."* packs a powerful punch of happiness. Maybe some of our goals should be based on the happiness of others instead of one's own happiness. Try it for a week.

3. **Power** *Bigger than You. You are Tiny. He is Huge.*

Never forget that God is bigger than you. And, He has made promises to you that ensure your happiness. He has told you that you will never be confronted with something you cannot handle. He has given you a way to communicate with Him. He has given you the power of prayer and the power of faith. I encourage you to start your day and end your day with communication with God. In the morning, the burden will lift from your heart and He will give you the power and the tools to tackle any obstacle the day may bring you. In the evening, say thank you for all the blessings you have received in the day. One of my favorite things to pray about is the happiness of my enemies. *"Lord, please let my boss who can find nothing good in me be happy."* Or, *"Lord please let the girl at school find happiness in ways other than gossiping and putting others down."* I challenge you to believe in prayer and say this prayer. The results are amazing!

Stop worrying! Worrying accomplishes absolutely nothing except to add stress and wrinkles to your life. Think about what you worry about. The majority of worries are about things you have no control over. If this is true in your life, re-read the section about healthy goals and apply it to your life. Worrying is part of being human but control the amount allowed in your life because it has absolutely no power. It's like a vacuum sucking the happiness out of your soul.

Several years ago while enjoying the weekend on the lake we tied the boat at the front and the back to trees, a common practice with the type of boat we had. One night with the boat tied up to a tree, a powerful storm came through. My husband jumped out of bed, cemented his rear end in the front of the boat not daring to remove his eye from the rope holding us to the tree. He sat there all night, never winking, and never returning to bed. I on the other hand, said a prayer and was back asleep in minutes. The boat never moved throughout the night. I had a full night's sleep while my husband was grumpy and tired the entire following day. The moral of the story: worrying doesn't do any good. Learn to let go.

Give thanks. Another simple concept but one we easily forget. We get so caught up in the "importance" and busyness of our lives that we sometimes forget to say thank you. Say thank you to those in your life, your family, your co-workers, your friends. Not only does it show compassion and bring smiles to those you are thanking but it brings happiness to you as well. Without God there would be no you so give Him thanks for all of your blessings.

4. **Play.** *Life is short so have some fun along the way.*

Move. Physical movement must be a part of your daily life. Being physically fit goes a long way to being mentally fit and achieving consistent happiness. Chemically, exercise alters your body by releasing endorphins, like little happy bugs throughout your entire body! When you finish a workout, you have a sense of accomplishment. And how happy are you when you see results like losing a couple of pounds or fitting in that pair of jeans you had given up on. Create a goal for yourself and start slowly, one step at a time, one day at a time.

Your support system is crucial to your happiness. The people we spend our time with and the activities we choose to partake in say everything you need to know about your priorities. Look at the people around you. Do they offer you encouragement? Do you laugh with them? Do they support your endeavors? Are they there to cry with? If the answer is no then you need to find new friends. One must be around positive people to stay positive. If you are in a negative relationship either change it or leave it.

How do you spend your time? Are you engaged in activities that bring you joy? Do you have trouble getting up in the morning because you dread going to work every day? Do you feel guilty about how you spend your time? Are you constantly thinking about other things you wish you could do? Answer these questions about your own life. Life is short so spend your time wisely. If you feel guilty or feel you are constantly chasing but never achieving then maybe you're spending your time doing things that aren't productive to your happiness.

You can't go through life alone. One of my personal symptoms of depression is the longing urge to be by myself. I have to tell myself to spend time with others and that isn't healthy. Create a happiness support system. Make it a priority to do at least a couple things within the structure of a group. Go to church and don't sit on the back pew and sneak out as soon as you hear the word Amen. Go to a weekly or monthly class with a friend. Occasionally, step out of your comfort zone and see what happens.

Smiling and laughter is the window letting light flow freely in and out of your heart. Isn't it cool when your face is sore because you've been laughing and smiling so much! We all need to lighten up and not take each other so seriously! We are all odd and unique individuals and we should celebrate these differences by sharing our experiences together. Have you ever been in a bad mood and made yourself start laughing. It's amazing because it becomes contagious and you are instantly in a better mood. It's proven that smiling and laughing have positive mental and physical impacts on the human body. Stress is released and again those friendly little endorphins invade us giving us energy and happiness. Your smile has the power to light up an entire room.

One of my favorite examples of the contagiousness of laughter happened only recently. I was driving down a busy street and had stopped at a red light. It was a bright sunny summer day and the top of the jeep was down so we could enjoy the sunshine to its fullest. My passenger for the excursion was my best friend. He happened to be in a rather sour mood caused from the normal stresses we all experience. I was determined to change his mood. So, while stopped at the intersection, top down on the jeep, cars on all sides, I started laughing out loud for no particular reason. My laughter was loud and goofy and soon those around started to stare and some started to laugh with me. My best friend started laughing too. His sour mood was gone and we were both smiling.

So pack your life with the Four P's: Power, Passion, Planning and Play. Open the door of your soul to the Lord by using these tools. Let Him create happiness in your heart and allow Him to make your happiness contagious to all around you.

13) My Favorite Person In The World

When I was a little girl I idolized my uncle and he was the "bestest" of the best. He was my Uncle and my Uncle alone. He belonged to me and nobody else. I didn't like to share my Uncle with anyone.

Uncle is my Mom's little brother. He was only four years old when my Mom and Dad got married. I think he got a good brunt of Grandpa's depressed moods aimed at him. Being the youngest, as a kid my Uncle was with Grandma and Grandpa alone much of the time. As such, my Mom and Dad took him under their wings and I guess in many ways my Mom has been more of a mother to him than a sister. Bubba and I got the benefits of this relationship because my Uncle spent a lot of time at our house. Even when my Uncle moved to another state for a job he would drive his motorcycle back to our house on the weekends and spend the entire time with us kids. He probably wasn't even 20 or 21 at the time so it was pretty cool that he spent so much time with us.

When he was away I would write him letters. Who knows what I wrote about! But he religiously wrote back. His dedication to us left a big imprint on my heart.

When he came home on the weekends our favorite activity was wrestling. My Mom usually was a spectator but my Uncle, Bubba, my Dad and I would make it an all-out war full of head locks, wet willies and several broken couches. Those memories are sublime and they always bring a smile to my face.

When I was in the fourth grade my Uncle had permanently moved back from living out of state and he started to date one particular girl quite a bit. Now, this was a problem for me because my Uncle was mine and mine alone. I was quite the jealous fourth grade girl. But things didn't change too much. Bubba and I continued to spend a lot of time together with my Uncle, often tagging along on his dates. Our favorite date nights were full of pizza or cashew chicken and miniature golf. Soon my Uncle married his girlfriend. Bubba and I were both in the wedding. I was overwhelmed with sadness thinking I was losing my Uncle forever and I had grown quite despiteful of his new bride!

It's funny because now as an adult I have a very good relationship with his wife and we've had many conversations reminiscing of those times. Come to find out she didn't really like me either at the time! She would have liked to have had some of those dates without us kids!

In my eyes my Uncle was flawless and could do no wrong. As a child, and for a long time as an adult I didn't know he suffered from depression like the rest of us. I would have never guessed it but when you idolize someone you usually don't see their shortcomings. He's very open about his experience and his struggle now. I reached out to him out of desperation when I was worried about Bubba. When I solicited his help he opened his heart. He was transparent and invited me into his world and his inner demons. His words helped me connect the dots between Grandpa, Bubba, me and the rest of the family.

My Uncle's depression had gotten so bad at one point that he plain didn't care. He just wanted to be left alone. He didn't care who he hurt or if he lost everything including his family. He had hit bottom and depression had taken over his life. Maybe this is how Grandpa felt but I can't grasp how it leads to suicide. I can see how you can push everyone out of your life but to want to be alone so much that you can only see relief through suicide completely bewilders me.

Have you ever watched that show about intervention? Well, it's kind of like that. You have to be confronted when you're at your very worst. He finally budged when his entire family, his wife and his kids unified, said they were done. They weren't kidding. They were going to leave. The ultimatum was to go to the doctor and get help or they were gone. Somewhere it nudged on a heart string because he agreed to it.

My Uncle acted like my Grandpa and Bubba. His depression seeped out of him in angry words and he retreated away from everyone. I didn't know about this side of his life because I didn't live with him. To me, he was simply my favorite person in the world, every time I saw him. See, no one knows about how depression affects people unless they live on the inside. No one knows about mine unless I tell them. Mine isn't about anger so even those closest to me sometimes cannot grasp the magnitude of how I suffer.

My uncle enlightened me when he explained how very fortunate he is that he said yes to his family and went to the doctor. He's convinced that if he had refused he would now be living completely depressed, completely alone. But he did say yes. He went to the doctor with his wife by his side. It was the only way he would. He didn't say but a few words while there. Instead his wife did the talking. He sat there and simply nodded. The key was he didn't feel like he was forced to do anything and he didn't have to leave his soul in that tiny room. Instead he left the room, his wife by his side, with the simple yet life changing willingness to try the doctor's recommendation.

I know that day saved his life. He would have been another Grandpa. If you ask him about it he'll talk to you but otherwise you'd never know. When he does talk he's shockingly honest. I believe that when we fall we also learn while getting up. I've learned a great deal from him and his willingness to be such an open book. I've been edified not only from his dark moments but also from his journey into the light.

He had been driven to his darkest moment. We should look at our shortcomings as opportunities for greatness. Do not let your depression, sadness or limitations drive you deeper down. Instead look at these moments and trials as ways to learn about yourself and to improve according to God's promises to you. God doesn't want you to be propelled by the negative. He wants you to be content and not to worry because He is the way through tribulations. *"I am not saying this because I am in need, for I have learned to be content whatever the circumstances. I know what it is to be in need, and I know what it is to have plenty. I have learned the secret of being content in any and every situation, whether well fed or hungry, whether living in plenty or in want. I can do all this through him who gives me strength,"* Philippians 4:11-13 NIV.

To me my Uncle epitomizes the fact that someone can be depressed and 99% of the world has no clue. Maybe I'm wearing rose colored glasses but he has always been very involved in church, at the center of his family and he has always excelled in his career. Unless you were in his ultimate inner circle witnessing his daily struggles and personally dealing with those symptoms you wouldn't have known.

In fact, I really didn't know for most of my life. I've learned most about his experience talking with him trying to make heads and tails of my own depression and my brother's experience. I really don't know the details and I do not need to. Those are for him and his family. What I do know is he finally came to the point where he

174

got help. I do know if you ask he will be completely open and honest with you. He will share the rawness. I would describe that as a story of triumph.

14) Let God In

We so often walk alone in our life when in reality helping hands surround us. Individuals in my family suffered silently when many were going through the exact same torments! Yet for so long we suffered silently and alone.

Do not be silent anymore! Just as I found relief by explaining my needs and struggles to my physician and through writing my book and blog, you can find relief too. Talk to your friends and family about your struggles. Your struggles and your sins are no greater or worse than theirs. Find comfort from one another. Lean on one another. *"Carry each other's burdens, and in this way you will fulfill the law of Christ. If anyone thinks he is something when he is nothing, he deceives himself. Each one should test his own actions. Then he can take pride in himself, without comparing himself to somebody else, for each one should carry his own load. Anyone who receives instruction in the word must share all good things with his instructor,"* Galatians 6:2-6 NIV.

Do not be afraid to share your trials and weaknesses with others. We aren't perfect. We are human. God sent His son to die on the cross so we don't have to be perfect. Why do we set such a humanized standard of perfection upon ourselves? It's unattainable and generally leads to grief and the feeling of failure. Yet, one of our weaknesses, at least one of my own, is the unwieldiness to admit our weaknesses and to ask for help. Isn't that what prayer is for? Aren't we told to be anxious of nothing? *"Be anxious for nothing, but in everything by prayer and supplication, with thanksgiving, let your requests be made known to God; and the peace of God, which surpasses all understanding, will guard your hearts and minds through Christ Jesus,"* Philippians 4:4-7 NASB.

Turning inward to deal with your grief only opens the door for Satan to utilize your affliction for his goals. Until you give your burdens to the Lord your sorrow only grows bigger.

Isn't that why we are also instructed to have a support system? *"Two are better than one because they have a good reward for their labor. For if they fall, one will life up his companion. But woe to him who is alone when he falls, for he has woe one to help him up. Again, if two lie down together, they will keep warm; but how can one be warm alone? Though one may be overpowered by another, two can withstand him. And a threefold cord is not quickly broken,"* Ecclesiastes 4:9-12 NASB.

Maybe it's time to examine how supportive your support system really is! Do you have real authentic friends who give you positive feedback and criticism? Do you feel free to share your struggles with them? Or do you fear judgment so you turn inward allowing depression and anxiety to grow? Surround yourself with people who lift you up and consistently are there to lend a hand. You don't have to have hundreds of people in your support system. You just need those in your support system who are strong enough to stand up for you and truly have your best interest at heart.

Do you have a church family? If not, I strongly encourage you to find one. I grew up in a family who went to church on Sunday morning, Sunday night and Wednesday evening. As an adult I've traveled my own path at times. At times that path has been very similar to my childhood pattern that my parents led me down and at times I've been pretty much completely off the church radar. I allowed myself to be off the radar due to selfishness. I had the false pretense that I could do it on my own. The introvert in me made it even harder to go back through the doors. However, every time I do I feel stronger. I feel re-charged. I feel supported. Make a commitment to it and make it a weekly goal. You'll be happy that you did!

How does one go about changing from depressed to joyful? Making a conscious decision to meditate on good things is a starting point. If you are busy thinking about happy things then you won't have the time, space or the energy for negative thoughts.

Make a plan. Start each day with reading a scripture. Sign up for one of those inspirational messages of the day emails. Write down five things you are thankful for every night before you close your eyes. When you feel negative thoughts coming on stop, breathe and pray.

Always look for the light of God and don't be afraid to shine your own light. The definition of light: *The natural agent that stimulates sight and makes things visible.* God has given you an internal light that is more radiant and more powerful than the beautiful sun we get to see daily. Make sure your authentic light shines throughout each day to bless those around you and watch the blessings flow to you!

When it comes down to it your walk in faith can be summarized by examining your personal relationship with God. Do you rely on Him to lead you? To comfort you? To bring you joy? To rebuke you?

How do you grow closer to God? You have to build a relationship with Him! This is not a hard concept – like always, I say keep it simple! Follow these four simple ideas to build your relationship with God on a daily basis.

1. Prayer – Talk to God. Talk to Him about everything – the good, the bad and the ugly!
2. Praise – Tell Him thank you for all the blessings he bestows on you. Thank Him for all the beauty in your life. Thank Him even for the struggles in your life and using them to grow closer to Him.
3. Pals – You must have friends in your life that have the same beliefs as you. You must have friends who will help you up when you fall, who will give you encouragement. You must have friends you can fellowship with.
4. Peruse – In order to have a relationship with Him, you must know Him. He's given us a tool for this and it's called the Bible. Peruse, read, and learn. Do it daily. Ask for guidance, inspiration and clarity when you read it.

15) Forward Motion

There are probably many people close to you, people you work with, people you go to school with, people you go to church with who are suffering from sadness, struggles and even depression. Anyone from any walk of life can be depressed. They may have the same symptoms as you do. Highly functional people can be depressed. Anyone can. At the time I was writing this book I was serving as the Director of Sales and Marketing for a large national resort where I served on the leadership team and was directly response for a staff of nearly 20. Do you think they knew I was depressed? I highly doubt it. I was the captain on my college volleyball team. Do you think my teammates or my coach knew I was depressed? Absolutely not.

Look at David in the Old Testament. He conquered thousands and is infamous for defeating the giant, Goliath. The Lord used him time and time again as a leader, charging in triumph over the enemy. So, how could someone who demonstrated such strength, power and leadership be depressed? Does it give you hope that He was chosen by God? Many psychology professionals today conjure that David was bipolar because of his many highs and lows.

I'm sure the soldiers under his demand didn't think he was depressed. In Judges it states that over 600 men were in David's army. David was a courageous warrior and, *"a man after God's own heart."* But in contrast, David also lived a life full of sadness, deeply grieving for his beloved friend Jonathan, King Saul and even his own sons. Of Jonathan, David spoke, *"My dear brother, I am crushed by your death, your friendship was a miracle, love far exceeding anything I have known or ever hope to know,"* 2 Samuel 1:26 MSG.

David could be a jubilant man, joyfully dancing before the Lord. On the flipside he was down trodden and deep in the threshold of depression, *"For when I kept silent, my bones wasted away through my groaning all day long. For day and night your hand was heavy upon me; my strength was dried up as by the heat of summer. I acknowledged my sin to you, and I did not cover my iniquity; I said, "I will confess my transgressions to the LORD," and you forgave the iniquity of my sin,"* Psalm 32:3-5 ESV.

No matter where you are on your life's journey you must live every moment to its fullest. Are you just going through the motions? It's easy to get tangled in this worldly jungle and forget that Jesus is in our midst. I encourage you to practice self-examination – inspect your life.

- Are you where you want to be?

- Do you feel fulfilled?

- Can you truly say you are happy?

- Do you feel at peace?

If your answer was no to the questions then ask yourself:

- Do you honestly take Jesus seriously?

- Do you really think He is in control?

- Do you think too much of yourself?

- Do you rely on your own understanding?

- Are you just going through the motions or are you truly committed to Him?

- Do you limit His mercy?

- Do you limit His grace?

- Is your faith limited?

Whether depressed and concentrated on putting one foot in front of the other or you're challenged with switching tracks to build a real relationship with God you should tell others about it. At the least tell your friends and support system. They'll be grateful to go on the journey with you. They will offer encouragement on days your faith wavers and you won't be able to hide!

"This is the beginning of a new day. You have been given this day

to use as you will. You can waste it or use it for good. What you do today is important because you are exchanging a day of your life for it. When tomorrow comes, this day will be gone forever; in its place is something that you have left behind… let it be something good," Author Unknown.

I'm so proud of my Uncle and Bubba and I know they are both better today than they were yesterday. They are great examples to future generations, sharing if you accept and acknowledge your depression or any hardship then you can escape its control. They've worked so hard to break our family curse and they've committed to it on a daily basis. They have their struggles but they are okay and they're going to make it.

I deal with my Grandpa's choices on a daily basis. Actually, I don't deal with them. I struggle with them. I think I will until the day I die. Even dealing with my own depression I can't begin to grasp or understand the choice of suicide. It has been over ten years since Grandpa made his choice. It still angers me. Everyone has had to deal with his choice except for him. Over ten years later we are still dealing with it.

I tell myself that I need to let it go. There is nothing to change the past. I can only look towards the future. Maybe in some obscure, sick way their choices opened the eyes of our future generations to avoid forthcoming tragedies. We have been able to recognize our own struggles and became brave enough to admit and cope with them. Maybe that wouldn't have happened otherwise. I don't know why it had to happen at all.

We can already see the curse spreading its seeds to the next generation. If they choose they have the tools, examples and support to control it. I don't want to be sitting on cold pews prematurely.

As for me, I get up every day and put one foot in front of the other. Some days it is easy and some days it is frighteningly hard. That's my reality. Life goes on day by day and hour by hour. We all grow older. Good and bad things happen to everyone.

This year marked the first year I've worried about my parents health and longevity. I was having a business lunch on the Friday of Fourth of July weekend when I heard my phone buzzing in my purse. I ignored it not wanting to be rude to my lunch guest. When I got to my car following lunch I dug my phone from the depths of my purse. Connected to my voice mail, I was greeted by my Mother's voice telling me that she had taken Dad to the hospital. He had not suffered a heart attack but something wasn't right so he had been admitted to the hospital. Over the next few days Dad had surgery to place stints in his almost closed arteries. The main heart attack causing artery was 99% blocked.

We all sat in the waiting room stunned. Dad is the personification of good health and only 60 some years young. He hadn't had any symptoms. He was just tired. The only reason he went to get checked out was because he had a softball tournament that weekend and Mom threatened that he wouldn't be able to play if he was so sleepy. There's a very good chance he would have suffered a heart attack on that ball field.

Dad's on a traveling softball team for guys 60 years and older. He plays basketball three times a week. He's tall and slender and eats like a bird. He doesn't drink and he doesn't smoke. No one would have guessed he was a walking heart attack set to go off.

It's the first time my parents' morbidity hit me in the face. My mind raced. What if he died? How would I react? How would Mom react? No, he can't die, God wouldn't do that to the grandkids. They couldn't cope. Mom's health is not good either. This conversation constantly ran through my mind for weeks.

What if Dad recovered but had to change his lifestyle? What if he couldn't be as active as he wanted to be? That's what happened to Grandpa. He couldn't handle it and killed himself. No, Dad wouldn't do that. Would he? He can handle it, right? No, I can't think about it. Everything will be okay. But will it really be okay?

It's been over a year since the surgery and dad is doing fine. There have been a few bumps in the road but overall everything is back to normal. Even with life being good, occasionally my mind wonders to those dark places where everything turns bad. If Dad has trouble again will he get depressed? He does have the tendency to get down on himself if he can't do what he wants to do. He loves playing ball. What will he do when he has to stop playing? This is how my mind operates. I have to physically tell it to stop or not only would I be depressed but I would be crazy too!

If you find yourself depressed, if you find yourself stricken with grief, if you find yourself just plain tired I encourage you to find strength in God's promises. He knows you. He lived here. He sent His son to live with us. Don't be shy! Ask Him to help! Look to the words of "East to West" by Casting Crowns for some inspiration.

"East to West"

Here I am, Lord, and I'm drowning in your sea of forgetfulness
The chains of yesterday surround me
I yearn for peace and rest
I don't want to end up where You found me
And it echoes in my mind, keeps me awake tonight
I know You've cast my sin as far as the east is from the west
And I stand before You now as though I've never sinned

But today I feel like I'm just one mistake away from You leaving
me this way

Jesus, can You show me just how far the east is from the west
'cause I can't bear to see the man I've been come rising
up in me again

In the arms of Your mercy I find rest
'cause You know just how far the east is from the west
From one scarred hand to the other...

16) Looking Forward

When you read Lamentations 21 and 22 you notice that Jeremiah was able to focus on his thoughts that were leading to his depression and once he recognized the patterns he was able to dig out of his depression hole. *"This I recall to my mind, therefore I have hope,"* Lamentations 3:21 NASB. We can learn from Jeremiah that recognition and discovery of our thinking patterns give us the ability to change and therefore have hope moving forward.

Once a thought pattern has changed from negative to positive it causes hope to grow in the heart. And, hope leads to faith. Trusting in the Lord and living life by faith leads to happiness.

Don't believe that I think escaping the destructive pattern of depression is easy! If it was easy and if it didn't afflict so many then God wouldn't have addressed it time and time again in the Bible. He wouldn't be known as the Counselor and Prince of Peace if He didn't realize the harm of depression and if He didn't care about us.

It takes a lot of work and determination to change your thinking patterns and your life habits. This is one my greatest struggles. It is so comforting and easy for me to draw into a shell just like a tortoise, avoiding social interaction. I must make plans for these interactions just like a mother would plan play dates for her kids. If I don't have a commitment and responsibility to someone else I can easily fall prey to the safety of my shell.

As I've had the blessing for more self-discovery during the process of writing this book I've realized how closely depression and the relief thereof are centered at the core of the Fruit of the Spirit. God must be pointing me in that direction because references keep popping up at every turn. I'm confident that the Fruit of the Spirit is a key to true happiness.

I don't know if I'll ever visit Grandpa's grave. If I was a betting woman I would say that I will. I'm just not for sure when. I was surprised to find out that my Mom has visited the grave. Her relationship with Grandpa has a much deeper history filled with questions and confusion – much more than mine. More emptiness too. There are so many questions that will probably never be answered. There are so many different opinions, memories and conflicting perspectives.

My Mom is the absolute most wonderful person on Earth. She brings a childlike spirit and glow which grows in any room she enters. She's infectious. Even with those wonderful, undeniable qualities she also is entangled in the family's web of depression. Hers comes in a very physical form. She is plagued with migraines, fibromyalgia and daily pain that most couldn't bear. Grandpa dealt with some of these demons and I'm now showing signs of the same. I am firmly convinced there is a connection.

Mom found the courage to visit that grave. I've yet to find it. Did it change anything? It didn't change the past events. It didn't change how depression leaves its impact on our lives, now or in the future. But, I think her heart is ever so slightly lighter and brighter. I think that makes it worth it. I hope to find the courage. I need to add that to my daily prayers.

Do you fight depression or self -doubt? Do you find yourself trying to live up to worldly standards? Remember the tools He has given you to battle these struggles:

1. You are made in the image of God. How can you not live up to the standard? How can you not be beautiful?

2. He will never give you more than you can handle. Whatever the mountain is before you He will either move it or help you climb it.

3. Look at all the tools He has given you: Prayer, Confession, the Holy Spirit, and the Bible. Pray

about your needs and your concerns. Confess you sins and your doubt. Ask for the Holy Spirit to intervene. And, get to know God and all he wants for you by reading the Bible.

4. You don't have to be perfect. That is not the expectation. The expectation is for you to accept His grace.

5. And, create a support system. Remember, that where ever more than one believer is gathered He is there.

In order to achieve true happiness one must put God's promises to work in their life. By doing so, God will never allow you to stumble. The easiest way to apply this is in your life is to focus on the fruit of the Spirit. The spirit consists of love, joy, peace, patience, kindness, goodness, faithfulness, gentleness and self-control.

This might seem to be a daunting task so I challenge you to attack this as you would any other goal in your life. You must make a plan and work the plan. It's not going to happen overnight. We must start reaching for our spiritual goals in the same manner in which we reach for worldly goals.

For example let's say you decide you want to run a marathon. Would you expect to be able to run that marathon the very next day? No way! So, why would you expect to achieve your spiritual goals overnight? The marathon runner would make a plan to run certain distances on a daily basis, slowly building up their stamina and their distance. This is how God wants you to build your spiritual knowledge and your relationship with Him.

You should make a plan so you are constantly "increasing in measure". Break your goals down into daily, weekly and monthly segments and measure your growth by your increasing insight and knowledge. Do this just like a runner would measure their increasing distance. Throughout this process you have to maintain perspective or else you'll lose confidence and motivation. Remember where you started, keep track of your progress and always make goals for the future.

When you slack in your performance, and you

will because you are human, remember that God has chosen you and He has a purpose just for you. In fact, wouldn't it be great to start off each morning reminding yourself that God chose you and He knows your purpose. Do this in the morning and then throughout the day. Be cognizant of how you are using the fruit of the spirit. At the end of the week, look back at your progress then make a plan for the next week. Always move forward!

What does it feel like to receive God's promises? How will your life change? The Bible describes the transformation as being born again. It's your chance to wipe the slate clean and to start completely over with the freedom that comes in a life lived with the Holy Spirit.

The Holy Spirit is the key and while the Holy Spirit can seem like this mysterious power or being I ask you to keep it simple. Just open your mind to the fact that the Holy Spirit has the key to unlock the door to living like God wants you to live. The Holy Spirit will give you guidance on how to live with the fruit of the Spirit as the foundation of your life and the Holy Spirit will let you experience the joy the fruit can give you.

I grew up going to church camp and one of the goofy songs we sang was about the fruit of the Spirit. It went something like this:

> *The fruit of the spirit's not an "apple" (you can insert any fruit you want)*
>
> *The fruit of the spirit's not an apple.*
>
> *If you want to be an apple you might as well hear it. You can't be a fruit of the Spirit.*
>
> *Cause the Spirit is love, joy, peace, patience, kindness, goodness, faithfulness, gentleness and self-control.*
>
> *Love, joy, peace, patience, kindness, goodness, faithfulness, gentleness and self-control. – Author Unknown*

Well, you better believe the fruit of the spirit doesn't include some depressed, bruised, pathetic and mushy banana! (By the way, I absolutely hate bananas!)

If you live a life led by your relationship with God then you should be producing His fruit. When people see you they should see His love illustrated by your actions. They should see a person who is full of love, joy, peace, patience, kindness, goodness, gentleness and self-control. Can a person with depression produce such fruit? I think it is possible. Will you produce the fruit God intends you to produce? If you've allowed your depression to control you and you struggle to hear God's voice in your life then I would say no.

When I imagine the fruit of the spirit I see them growing on a huge beautiful oak. The tree is strong, with deep roots and a towering trunk. Its limbs are far reaching and no matter the season it stands for all to see. What would the opposite of this scene look like? In the Bible God uses weeds to describe the power of sin. If you aren't producing Godly fruit then you are producing sinful fruit. I see a wrangled long, but strong weed that wraps and entangles around all it comes in contact. As it multiplies in strength and force it chokes the life out of those it suffocates. On occasion you try and kill the weed by pulling it from the ground or cutting it off but it seems to always find its way back. What would this weed or this fruit look like in your life? I think it would be the exact opposite of the fruit of the spirit.

Fruit vs. Weeds (opposites)

Love vs. Hate

Joy vs. Sorrow

Peace vs. Warfare

Patience vs. Agitation

Kindness vs. Cruelty

Goodness vs. Badness

Faithfulness vs. Negligence

Gentleness vs. Hardness

Self-Control vs. Rashness

Aren't these some of the symptoms and behaviors a depressed person shows? I certainly display them in my life. Depression can be like a weed strangling out your energy, your vitality and your will and replacing it with agitation, negligence and hardness. The weeds are not easy to exhume. Think of how hard a farmer toils to produce good fruit! You have to tend to it daily and constantly create barriers blocking the weeds. This is how depression is! You have to diligently work to control it and not be controlled by it. But, it is possible. God wants you to produce His fruit! You can do it!

Being sad or even clinically depressed is okay! Being depressed is not a sin. However, it's not okay to let sadness or depression rule your life. You don't want to live that way. God doesn't want you to live that way. Whether you are suffering from clinical depression, if you're grieving over a loss, or going through a personal trial – all of which can be natural periods of human life they should have a definitive time frame. Jesus experienced all of these too! They are normal processes and experiences. However, if you let them linger too long they eventually rule your life. Jesus never grieved for long and you shouldn't either. I really don't care if you are mopey, dopey, down, down and out, depressed, dejected, sad, whiny, anxious, having a rough time of it or whatever word or phrase you wish to use! God didn't create you to be like that!

Jesus is there for you in this very moment. What is Jesus doing right now? I was recently reading a book and it made me think about what Jesus is doing. I've never thought about it before! He died on the cross for the forgiveness of our sins and stated, *"It is finished."* He doesn't need to do anything for our sins because it has already been done. *"Therefore he is able, once and forever, to save those who come to God through him. He lives forever to intercede with God on their behalf,"* – Hebrews 7:25 NLT.

So what is He doing now? The answer is He is constantly interceding for you!

1. When you are worried He intercedes for you.
2. When you don't know what to say He intercedes for you.
3. When you are nervous He intercedes for you.
4. When you are angry He intercedes for you.
5. When you are sad He intercedes for you.
6. When you are disappointed He intercedes for you.

7. When you are scared He intercedes for you.

8. When you are confused He intercedes for you.

9. When you are lonely He intercedes for you.

10. When you are worried He intercedes for you.

11. When you are depressed He intercedes for you.

"And he that searcheth the hearts knoweth what is *the mind of the Spirit, because he maketh intercession for the saints according to the will of God. And we know that all things work together for good to them that love God, to them who are the called according to* His *purpose,"* Romans 8:27-29 KJV.

Read the following verse and then say it out loud: *"I can do all things through Christ who strengthens me,"* Philippians 4:13 NASB. This is a very simple statement but do you really believe it? Do you have dreams that you haven't reached for? Does fear hold you back from change? Are you in a job that you can't stand? Do you have toxic friends yet fail to end the relationships?

Life is frail and life is very short, however, most of us go through the daily grind, unwilling to make any changes about all of our grumblings. The only choice we make is to continue grumbling. Most of us fear change, even if the change would bring positivity and goodness to our life.

What is holding you back? Do you think you aren't good enough? *"For you formed my inward parts; you knitted me together in my mother's womb. I praise you, for I am fearfully and wonderfully made. Wonderful are your works; my soul knows it very well,"* Psalm 139:13-14 ESV.

Do you simply not have the courage? *"Have I not commanded you? Be strong and courageous. Do not be frightened, and do not be dismayed, for the LORD your God is with you wherever you go,"* Joshua 1:9 ESV.

Are you not willing to find the time and put forth the effort, busying yourself with things that don't matter? *"Therefore I tell you, do not worry about your life, what you will eat or drink; or about your body, what you will wear. Is not life more important than food, and the body more important than clothes? Look at the birds of the air; they do not sow or reap or store away in barns, and yet your heavenly Father feeds them.*

Are you not much more valuable than they? Who of you by worrying can add a single hour to his life?

"And why do you worry about clothes? See how the lilies of the field grow. They do not labor or spin. Yet I tell you that not even Solomon in all his splendor was dressed like one of these. If that is how God clothes the grass of the field, which is here today and tomorrow is thrown into the fire, will he not much more clothe you, O you of little faith? So do not worry, saying, 'What shall we eat?' or 'What shall we drink?' or 'What shall we wear?' For the pagans run after all these things, and your heavenly Father knows that you need them. But seek first his kingdom and his righteousness, and all these things will be given to you as well. Therefore do not worry about tomorrow, for tomorrow will worry about itself. Each day has enough trouble of its own," Matthew 6:24-34.

Do you just fear the unknown? *"For God has not given us a spirit of fear and timidity, but of power, love, and self-discipline,"* 2 Timothy 1:7.

Throw these excuses down the drain and never let fear hold you back again. Do it now! Make plans for your future. A future where God holds your hands, giving you hope every step of the way. *"For I know the plans I have for you," declares the LORD, "plans to prosper you and not to harm you, plans to give you hope and a future,"* Jeremiah 29:11 NIV.

This process has changed my focus from inward to outward. I have my struggles and downfalls like everyone. I am still a sinner but I'm happy and God is leading my life. It's time to take off the mask and master your insecurities. False fronts and deceptive emotions must be replaced with simple honesty. Defense mechanisms must be replaced with activity. Depression must be replaced with a plan for happiness.

It's so hard to jump sometimes. I guess that's why faith can be so hard to grasp. While writing this book I've drawn strength from my faith, albeit sometimes faltering faith, that this book will help people, that my family will be supportive, and that this is the path God wants me on. I do fully believe all of these. But, daily I reaffirm my faith by talking with God and reading His word and being around those who truly support me.

I can firmly say I am happier and stand on a better foundation than at the beginning of this journey. Through self-examination I have let go of past grievances and I have rediscovered my strengths and weaknesses making me better prepared to handle my journey through depression and my journey through life. I hope you are too!

I dare you to jump today into the arms of the Lord and to the life He has planned for you! Jump! He's waiting for you.

God grant me the serenity to accept the things I cannot change, the courage to change the things I can, and the wisdom to know the difference. Living one day at a time; enjoying one moment at a time; accepting hardship as the pathway to peace. Taking as He did, this sinful world as it is, not as I would have it. Trusting that He will make all things right if I surrender to His will. That I may be reasonably happy in this life, and supremely happy with Him forever in the next.

Notes

Chapter 5, Page 46

[1] Richard Winter, *When Life Goes Dark, 2012* (Downers Grove, Illinois: Intervarsity Press), pg. 80.

Chapter 7, Page 80

[1] Richard O'Conner, PhD, Undoing Depression - What Therapy Doesn't Teach You and Medication Can't Give You (Canada: Little, Brown and Company) pg. 4.

ABOUT THE AUTHOR

Jana, The Author - My name is Jana and God has blessed me in many ways. Parents who are always supportive, an absolutely wonderful brother and sister-n-law whom I love to death, two silly nephews who amaze me daily, my best friend and soul mate in life and last but not least three furry dogs whom I adore. I've grown up going to church and I've had great leaders and teachers pointing the way toward God. As an adult, I am now truly seeing the great wonders in having a personal relationship with Him.

I'm at the point in my life where I don't want to waste another minute. My goals are to consistently reach thousands of people and provide comfort, inspiration and guidance to a better life along the way. I'm currently working on three books, speaking engagements and a jewelry line. Updates on these endeavors can be found at www.ALightFilledLife.com.

Jana, The Child of God - I've been blessed to have wonderful spiritual leaders in my life and my foundation for my walk with God has and will always be my parents. They've taught me by study, fellowship and most importantly action in their own lives what being a Christian is really about, your relationship with God.

As in every relationship, my relationship with God has traveled from smooth sailing to rocky roads and back again. But no matter what He is my Rock that helps me overcome mountains. He is always there for me. He always listens. He is always compassionate. Even when I fail Him, He is there for me. My faith will forever reside in Him.

Jana, The Depressed - We all have different struggles we deal with on a daily or regular basis. One of my struggles is depression. Depression rears its head in my life in the way of seclusion and irritability. This might not sound too life altering but coming from a family where depression is genetic and depression has led to multiple suicides it's a struggle I take very seriously. Both of my grandfathers committed suicide. I pray for wisdom in how to deal with it. I pray that the symptoms lessen overtime. I pray that it doesn't affect those around me.

When I started studying and writing about my family's journey it opened the door to happiness. It has served as a sort of therapy for me. I've had to analyze my own good and bad parts. Self-inflection, if led by growth and change can be an energizing event. My blog was the ultimate turning point. It gave me goals and accountability. It gave me purpose. It took my focus off of me and onto others. It gave me excitement! I'm happy to share this journey with you and I hope we can learn from each other as we go!